LIVING LITURGY™

FOR
CANTORS

LIVING LITURGY™

FOR
CANTORS

Year C • 2016

Kathleen Harmon, S.N.D. de N.
Joyce Ann Zimmerman, C.PP.S.
Rev. John W. Tonkin

LITURGICAL PRESS
Collegeville, Minnesota

www.litpress.org

Design by Ann Blattner. Art by Martin Erspamer, OSB.

ISSN 1947-2862

ISBN 978-0-8146-4972-5

Presented to

---

in grateful appreciation
for ministering as a Cantor

(date)

USING THIS RESOURCE

Living Liturgy™ for Cantors is intended to help psalmists prepare themselves to sing the responsorial psalm by reflecting on the text of the psalm in the context of the readings of the day and applying this reflection to a spirituality for daily living. A cantor who has a sense of how the psalm is connected to the readings and to his or her daily living will sing the psalm with greater sensitivity. The cantor's singing will flow out of personal encounter with God, who works through the Liturgy of the Word to draw the cantor and the assembly more fully into being who they are: the Body of Christ.

Living Liturgy™ for Cantors contains the gospel readings, first readings, and responsorial psalms for every Sunday of the liturgical year, for those solemnities that are holy days of obligation, and for Ash Wednesday. An appendix contains the second readings for those days (namely, the Sundays of Advent, Christmas, Lent, and Easter; the solemnities; and Ash Wednesday) when that reading has an intended connection to the other readings. For each Sunday or solemnity the book provides a brief reflection on the gospel, a section connecting the psalm to the readings, a suggestion to help the psalmist prepare spiritually to sing the psalm, and a prayer drawn from the readings and the psalm.

While this book is a small one, it offers a wealth of preparatory material for the cantor of the psalm. Cantors might find the following method helpful in using this book and should feel free to adapt the method or to create another one to suit their needs and situation.

On Monday, read the gospel and spend some time reflecting on its meaning. Ask yourself who Jesus is in this gospel and what he is saying or doing. Who are we, and what are we saying or doing?

On Tuesday, read the first reading. Ask yourself who God is in this reading and what God is saying or doing. Who are we, and what are we saying or doing? Read "Reflecting on Living the Gospel" and see what further insights open up for you.

On Wednesday, look at the text of the psalm and see how it is connected to the readings. During the festal seasons of Advent, Christmas, Lent, and Easter, and for those days that are solemnities, read the second reading.

On Thursday, read "Connecting the Responsorial Psalm to the Readings" and "Psalmist Preparation" and decide how you might implement the suggested spirituality.

On Friday, sing through the psalm, letting your reflection and your daily living add a new dimension to your understanding of the text. Pray the suggested prayer and ask for the grace to do your ministry well.

On Saturday and Sunday, give yourself over to Christ so that he may be the voice the assembly hears.

Even more important than musical preparation of the psalm setting is the cantor's prayerful reflection on the meaning of the text and its role in his or her daily living. The cantor who does this kind of preparation discovers that his or her singing is a dialogue with God that mirrors the dialogue going on between God and the assembly in the Liturgy of the Word. A dimension opens up in the cantor's singing that is far deeper than the beauty of his or her voice. What the assembly hears is the cantor's surrender of self to the paschal mystery of Christ, and it is this surrender to which they respond.

Gospel (Luke 21:25-28, 34-36; L3C)

Jesus said to his disciples: "There will be signs in the sun, the moon, and the stars, and on earth nations will be in dismay, perplexed by the roaring of the sea and the waves. People will die of fright in anticipation of what is coming upon the world, for the powers of the heavens will be shaken. And then they will see the Son of Man coming in a cloud with power and great glory. But when these signs begin to happen, stand erect and raise your heads because your redemption is at hand.

"Beware that your hearts do not become drowsy from carousing and drunkenness and the anxieties of daily life, and that day catch you by surprise like a trap. For that day will assault everyone who lives on the face of the earth. Be vigilant at all times and pray that you have the strength to escape the tribulations that are imminent and to stand before the Son of Man."

First Reading (Jer 33:14-16)

The days are coming, says the LORD, when I will fulfill the promise I made to the house of Israel and Judah. In those days, in that time, I will raise up for David a just shoot; he shall do what is right and just in the land. In those days Judah shall be safe and Jerusalem shall dwell secure; this is what they shall call her: "The LORD our justice."

Responsorial Psalm (Ps 25:4-5, 8-9, 10, 14)

℟. (1b) To you, O Lord, I lift my soul.

Your ways, O LORD, make known to me;
    teach me your paths,
guide me in your truth and teach me,
    for you are God my savior,
    and for you I wait all the day.

℟. To you, O Lord, I lift my soul.

Good and upright is the LORD;
    thus he shows sinners the way.

He guides the humble to justice,
and teaches the humble his way.

℞. To you, O Lord, I lift my soul.

All the paths of the LORD are kindness and constancy
toward those who keep his covenant and his decrees.
The friendship of the LORD is with those who fear him,
and his covenant, for their instruction.

℞. To you, O Lord, I lift my soul.

See Appendix, p. 207, for Second Reading

Reflecting on Living the Gospel

At first reading, it seems as though the gospel is only about tribulations and calamities and fear. Yes, right now, today, tribulations, wars, natural calamities are upon us. We can cringe in fear or "stand erect" in hope. Jesus tells us not to fear what calamities might do to us, but to be "vigilant" for his coming. He comes with redemption not only in glory at the end of time but right now, today.

Connecting the Responsorial Psalm to the Readings

In these verses from Psalm 25 we beg God to teach us the way we should go. The word "way" refers not only to a path one is walking but also to a habitual manner of acting. We pray in this psalm, then, to walk in the direction God is pointing by living and acting as God does. This means doing what is "right and just" (first reading), conducting ourselves as Christ has instructed (second reading), and staying vigilant for Christ's coming (gospel). As we walk this way, we know God will guide our steps and surround us with "friendship" (psalm). On this first Sunday of a new liturgical year, we "stand erect" (gospel), lifting our souls to the God who is leading us in love to the fullness of Life.

Psalmist Preparation

In this psalm you ask God to teach you a way that is far more than a set of rules. You ask to be formed in "ways" of goodness, uprightness, constancy, and fidelity. In other words, you ask that your behavior become like God's. How might this prayer deepen your humility? How might it shape your living of Advent?

Prayer

Gracious God, you teach us the path of life. Keep us faithful to your way of living that we may one day bring your kingdom to completion and run with joy to greet Christ at his coming. We ask this in his name. Amen.

Gospel (Luke 3:1-6; L6C)

In the fifteenth year of the reign of
Tiberius Caesar, when Pontius Pilate was governor of
Judea, and Herod was tetrarch of Galilee, and his
brother Philip tetrarch of the region of
Ituraea and Trachonitis, and Lysanias was
tetrarch of Abilene, during the high priesthood
of Annas and Caiaphas, the word of God came to
John the son of Zechariah in the desert. John went
throughout the whole region of the Jordan,
proclaiming a baptism of repentance for the forgiveness of sins, as it is written in the book of the words of
the prophet Isaiah:

A voice of one crying out in the desert:
"Prepare the way of the Lord,
  make straight his paths.
Every valley shall be filled
  and every mountain and hill shall be made low.
The winding roads shall be made straight,
  and the rough ways made smooth,
and all flesh shall see the salvation of God."

First Reading (Bar 5:1-9)

Jerusalem, take off your robe of mourning and misery;
  put on the splendor of glory from God forever:
wrapped in the cloak of justice from God,
  bear on your head the mitre
  that displays the glory of the eternal name.
For God will show all the earth your splendor:
  you will be named by God forever
  the peace of justice, the glory of God's worship.

Up, Jerusalem! stand upon the heights;
  look to the east and see your children
gathered from the east and the west
  at the word of the Holy One,
  rejoicing that they are remembered by God.

Led away on foot by their enemies they left you:
　　but God will bring them back to you
　　borne aloft in glory as on royal thrones.
For God has commanded
　　that every lofty mountain be made low,
and that the age-old depths and gorges
　　be filled to level ground,
　　that Israel may advance secure in the glory of God.
The forests and every fragrant kind of tree
　　have overshadowed Israel at God's command;
for God is leading Israel in joy
　　by the light of his glory,
　　with his mercy and justice for company.

Responsorial Psalm (Ps 126:1-2, 2-3, 4-5, 6)

℟. (3) The Lord has done great things for us; we are filled with joy.

When the LORD brought back the captives of Zion,
　　we were like men dreaming.
Then our mouth was filled with laughter,
　　and our tongue with rejoicing.

℟. The Lord has done great things for us; we are filled with joy.

Then they said among the nations,
　　"The LORD has done great things for them."
The LORD has done great things for us;
　　we are glad indeed.

℟. The Lord has done great things for us; we are filled with joy.

Restore our fortunes, O LORD,
　　like the torrents in the southern desert.
Those who sow in tears
　　shall reap rejoicing.

℟. The Lord has done great things for us; we are filled with joy.

Although they go forth weeping,
　　carrying the seed to be sown,
they shall come back rejoicing,
　　carrying their sheaves.

℟. The Lord has done great things for us; we are filled with joy.

See Appendix, p. 207, for Second Reading

Reflecting on Living the Gospel
The meandering paths and winding roads of our lives are straightened and the valleys filled and mountains brought low when our lives are characterized by attitudes of repentance. Our work of repentance is a matter of turning ourselves toward the God who embraces us in mercy and forgiveness and welcomes us home. Our work of repentance is our response to the word-invitation to "see the salvation of God." We are to hear the "word of God" and act on it. Do we? How well?

Connecting the Responsorial Psalm to the Readings
When God delivered Israel from their captivity in Babylon, they responded with the creation of Psalm 126. Over time they came to use this psalm as a song of confidence any time they were in danger of destruction. The text moves from memorial of past deliverance (stanzas 1 and 2) to petition for new deliverance (stanzas 3 and 4). Israel's confidence was based on real historical events, not dreamed imaginings. Of this they were certain: the God who *had* saved them *would* save them again.

This too is our confidence as we journey through the season of Advent. We hear of restoration to come (first reading) and of salvation to be completed (second reading). With the Israelites we know our hope is not an empty dream but a realistic vision of what God will accomplish when Christ comes at last. We stand in the desert of Advent, but we dance with hope and joy.

Psalmist Preparation
In this responsorial psalm you call the community to the long view of history, telling them to imagine the future by remembering what God has done in the past. You remind them that the God who *has* saved *will* save again. Your singing expresses the messianic hope of the church. Who and what helps keep this hope alive in you? When your hope flags, who and what revives it for you?

Prayer
Redeeming God, you are the Lord of history. Fill our dreams with your vision of the future, and fill our hearts with steadfast confidence that your promise of salvation will be fulfilled for us in real time and place. We ask this through Christ our Lord. Amen.

Gospel (Luke 1:26-38; L689)

The angel Gabriel was sent from God to a town of Galilee called Nazareth, to a virgin betrothed to a man named Joseph, of the house of David, and the virgin's name was Mary. And coming to her, he said, "Hail, full of grace! The Lord is with you." But she was greatly troubled at what was said and pondered what sort of greeting this might be. Then the angel said to her, "Do not be afraid, Mary, for you have found favor with God. Behold, you will conceive in your womb and bear a son, and you shall name him Jesus. He will be great and will be called Son of the Most High, and the Lord God will give him the throne of David his father, and he will rule over the house of Jacob forever, and of his Kingdom there will be no end." But Mary said to the angel, "How can this be, since I have no relations with a man?" And the angel said to her in reply, "The Holy Spirit will come upon you, and the power of the Most High will overshadow you. Therefore the child to be born will be called holy, the Son of God. And behold, Elizabeth, your relative, has also conceived a son in her old age, and this is the sixth month for her who was called barren; for nothing will be impossible for God." Mary said, "Behold, I am the handmaid of the Lord. May it be done to me according to your word." Then the angel departed from her.

First Reading (Gen 3:9-15, 20)

After the man, Adam, had eaten of the tree, the LORD God called to the man and asked him, "Where are you?" He answered, "I heard you in the garden; but I was afraid, because I was naked, so I hid myself." Then he asked, "Who told you that you were naked? You have eaten, then, from the tree of which I had forbidden you to eat!" The man replied, "The woman whom you put here with me—she gave me fruit from the tree, and so I ate it." The LORD God then asked the woman, "Why did you do such a thing?" The woman answered, "The serpent tricked me into it, so I ate it."

Then the LORD God said to the serpent:

"Because you have done this, you shall be banned
    from all the animals
    and from all the wild creatures;

on your belly shall you crawl,
>and dirt shall you eat
>all the days of your life.
I will put enmity between you and the woman,
>and between your offspring and hers;
he will strike at your head,
>while you strike at his heel."

The man called his wife Eve, because she became the mother of all the living.

Responsorial Psalm (Ps 98:1, 2-3, 3-4)

R℣. (1a) Sing to the Lord a new song, for he has done marvelous deeds.

Sing to the LORD a new song,
>for he has done wondrous deeds;
his right hand has won victory for him,
>his holy arm.

R℣. Sing to the Lord a new song, for he has done marvelous deeds.

The LORD has made his salvation known:
>in the sight of the nations he has revealed his justice.
He has remembered his kindness and his faithfulness
>toward the house of Israel.

R℣. Sing to the Lord a new song, for he has done marvelous deeds.

All the ends of the earth have seen
>the salvation by our God.
Sing joyfully to the LORD, all you lands;
>break into song; sing praise.

R℣. Sing to the Lord a new song, for he has done marvelous deeds.

See Appendix, p. 207, for Second Reading

Reflecting on Living the Gospel

Mary responded to God's call to salvation by saying yes to the mystery of being overshadowed by the Holy Spirit and giving birth to the Son of God. We, too, respond to God's call to salvation by listening to the Spirit who dwells within us, by bearing Christ in the world today, by speaking an ongoing yes to whatever God asks of us. The mystery we live is the mystery of God's loving, saving, incarnate Presence.

THE IMMACULATE CONCEPTION OF THE BLESSED VIRGIN MARY

Connecting the Responsorial Psalm to the Readings

Adam and Eve turn away from God in disobedience (first reading). God does not respond, however, by turning away from the human family. Instead God works "marvelous deeds" on our behalf (psalm). On this solemnity we celebrate the marvelous deed that God preserved Mary free from all sin in preparation for her role as the new Eve who would bear Christ. We celebrate the marvelous deed that through Christ we have received adoption as God's very own children (second reading). We celebrate the marvelous deed of grace that enabled Mary to say yes to God, reversing the no of the first humans in the garden (gospel). No wonder we "Sing . . . a new song" (psalm) about all the things God does!

Psalmist Preparation

In response to human sin and infidelity God works marvelous deeds of salvation. Where do you see God's saving deeds in your own life? in the life of your family? in the life of the world community? How every day can you sing a new song to the Lord for these marvelous deeds?

Prayer

God of marvelous deeds, you adopt us in Christ as your sons and daughters. May we, like Mary, always say yes to the call of your will and the workings of your grace. We ask this in his name. Amen.

Gospel (Luke 3:10-18; L9C)

The crowds asked John the Baptist, "What should we do?" He said to them in reply, "Whoever has two cloaks should share with the person who has none. And whoever has food should do likewise." Even tax collectors came to be baptized and they said to him, "Teacher, what should we do?" He answered them, "Stop collecting more than what is prescribed." Soldiers also asked him, "And what is it that we should do?" He told them, "Do not practice extortion, do not falsely accuse anyone, and be satisfied with your wages."

Now the people were filled with expectation, and all were asking in their hearts whether John might be the Christ. John answered them all, saying, "I am baptizing you with water, but one mightier than I is coming. I am not worthy to loosen the thongs of his sandals. He will baptize you with the Holy Spirit and fire. His winnowing fan is in his hand to clear his threshing floor and to gather the wheat into his barn, but the chaff he will burn with unquenchable fire." Exhorting them in many other ways, he preached good news to the people.

First Reading (Zeph 3:14-18a)

Shout for joy, O daughter Zion!
  Sing joyfully, O Israel!
Be glad and exult with all your heart,
  O daughter Jerusalem!
The LORD has removed the judgment against you,
  he has turned away your enemies;
the King of Israel, the LORD, is in your midst,
  you have no further misfortune to fear.
On that day, it shall be said to Jerusalem:
  Fear not, O Zion, be not discouraged!
The LORD, your God, is in your midst,
  a mighty savior;
he will rejoice over you with gladness,
  and renew you in his love,
he will sing joyfully because of you,
  as one sings at festivals.

Responsorial Psalm (Isa 12:2-3, 4, 5-6)

℟. (6) Cry out with joy and gladness: for among you is the great and
Holy One of Israel.

God indeed is my savior;
    I am confident and unafraid.
My strength and my courage is the LORD,
    and he has been my savior.
With joy you will draw water
    at the fountain of salvation.

℟. Cry out with joy and gladness: for among you is the great and Holy
One of Israel.

Give thanks to the LORD, acclaim his name;
    among the nations make known his deeds,
    proclaim how exalted is his name.

℟. Cry out with joy and gladness: for among you is the great and Holy
One of Israel.

Sing praise to the LORD for his glorious achievement;
    let this be known throughout all the earth.
Shout with exultation, O city of Zion,
    for great in your midst
    is the Holy One of Israel!

℟. Cry out with joy and gladness: for among you is the great and Holy
One of Israel.

See Appendix, p. 207, for Second Reading

Reflecting on Living the Gospel
John the Baptist challenged the people who asked him, "What should we
do?" by admonishing them to far exceed their present way of acting
toward others. Yet even such "good news" does not measure up to what
the "one mightier" than John will ask of us: to live a Gospel that exacts
the gift of our very selves. If we ask, "What should we do?" we must be
prepared for an answer that challenges us. Are we willing even to ask the
question?

Connecting the Responsorial Psalm to the Readings

Instead of psalm verses this Sunday we sing a hymn from Isaiah proclaiming that the Holy One we await is already in our midst. The first and second readings affirm God is already present among us. John the Baptist announces the imminent arrival of the "one mightier than I" (gospel). No wonder we shout, "Cry out with joy and gladness" (psalm refrain)!

All is not joy and gladness, however. The very nearness of the Holy One makes our own unholiness more evident. We must change our behavior, for the coming Messiah will sort the wheat from the chaff and burn what he does not want (gospel). John's audience hears the call to conversion and the imminence of judgment as "good news" that heralds the coming of the Holy One of Israel. They hear that God's promise to renew them as a chosen people (first reading) is about to be fulfilled. What do we hear in John the Baptist's challenge? What response do we make, both in sung word and in lived behavior?

Psalmist Preparation

In these verses you are the prophet Isaiah announcing God's saving presence in the midst of the people. Even more, you are the church proclaiming the Holy One in our midst to be Jesus who saves us through the paschal mystery of his death and resurrection. How can your singing lead the assembly to see and encounter this Presence?

Prayer

Redeeming God, you send your prophets to announce your saving presence. Open our ears to hear the Good News of your coming, and give us the strength we need to undergo the changes necessary to make your presence known to all. We ask this through Christ our Lord. Amen.

Gospel (Luke 1:39-45; L12C)

Mary set out and traveled to the hill country in haste to a town of Judah, where she entered the house of Zechariah and greeted Elizabeth. When Elizabeth heard Mary's greeting, the infant leaped in her womb, and Elizabeth, filled with the Holy Spirit, cried out in a loud voice and said, *"Blessed are you among women, and blessed is the fruit of your womb.* And how does this happen to me, that the mother of my Lord should come to me? For at the moment the sound of your greeting reached my ears, the infant in my womb leaped for joy. Blessed are you who believed that what was spoken to you by the Lord would be fulfilled."

First Reading (Mic 5:1-4a)

Thus says the Lord:
You, Bethlehem-Ephrathah
    too small to be among the clans of Judah,
from you shall come forth for me
    one who is to be ruler in Israel;
whose origin is from of old,
    from ancient times.
Therefore the Lord will give them up, until the time
    when she who is to give birth has borne,
and the rest of his kindred shall return
    to the children of Israel.
He shall stand firm and shepherd his flock
    by the strength of the Lord,
    in the majestic name of the Lord, his God;
and they shall remain, for now his greatness
    shall reach to the ends of the earth;
    he shall be peace.

Responsorial Psalm (Ps 80:2-3, 15-16, 18-19)

R̠. (4) Lord, make us turn to you; let us see your face and we shall be saved.
O shepherd of Israel, hearken,
    from your throne upon the cherubim, shine forth.

Rouse your power,
  and come to save us.

R̸. Lord, make us turn to you; let us see your face and we shall be saved.

Once again, O LORD of hosts,
  look down from heaven, and see;
take care of this vine,
  and protect what your right hand has planted,
  the son of man whom you yourself made strong.

R̸. Lord, make us turn to you; let us see your face and we shall be saved.

May your help be with the man of your right hand,
  with the son of man whom you yourself made strong.
Then we will no more withdraw from you;
  give us new life, and we will call upon your name.

R̸. Lord, make us turn to you; let us see your face and we shall be saved.

See Appendix, p. 208, for Second Reading

Reflecting on Living the Gospel
Salvation is the convergence of God's will and our own will. Like Mary
and Elizabeth, we must always say yes to what God asks of us. Mary
and Elizabeth show us the way to *our* being overshadowed by the Spirit,
for they offered their own bodies in cooperating with God's plan of salvation. So must we offer ourselves with the same willingness, with the
same love response, with the same eager desire for divine Presence
within and among us.

Connecting the Responsorial Psalm to the Readings
In this responsorial psalm we beg God, "let us see your face and we shall
be saved." Where, in response, does God call us to look? Beyond the face
of the newborn Jesus to the face of the grown Christ carrying out God's
will (second reading). And through the face of Christ to the faces of one
another who, "consecrated" through Christ's offering, are now the Body
of Christ continuing to shine the face of salvation upon the world. In this
Sunday's liturgy we celebrate God's incarnation in human flesh—
Christ's, Mary's, and ours. Beyond all expectation, God has indeed heard
our prayer; beyond all expectation, God has indeed shown us the divine
face!

Psalmist Preparation

In this responsorial psalm you express the assembly's desire to turn more fully toward God. You lead them in begging to see God's face. How during this last week of Advent might you turn more toward God? Where might you look to see God's face? How might you be God's face for someone else?

Prayer

Shepherd of Israel, you shine the light of your face upon us. Keep us turned toward you that we may see your presence and rejoice in your salvation. We ask this through Christ our Lord. Amen.

Gospel **(Matt 1:1-25 [or Matt 1:18-25]; L13 ABC)**

The book of the genealogy of Jesus Christ, the son of David, the son of Abraham.

Abraham became the father of Isaac, Isaac the father of Jacob, Jacob the father of Judah and his brothers. Judah became the father of Perez and Zerah, whose mother was Tamar. Perez became the father of Hezron, Hezron the father of Ram, Ram the father of Amminadab. Amminadab became the father of Nahshon, Nahshon the father of Salmon, Salmon the father of Boaz, whose mother was Rahab. Boaz became the father of Obed, whose mother was Ruth. Obed became the father of Jesse, Jesse the father of David the king.

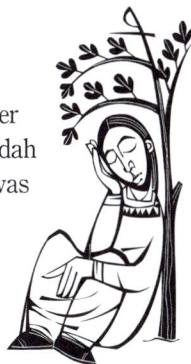

David became the father of Solomon, whose mother had been the wife of Uriah. Solomon became the father of Rehoboam, Rehoboam the father of Abijah, Abijah the father of Asaph. Asaph became the father of Jehoshaphat, Jehoshaphat the father of Joram, Joram the father of Uzziah. Uzziah became the father of Jotham, Jotham the father of Ahaz, Ahaz the father of Hezekiah. Hezekiah became the father of Manasseh, Manasseh the father of Amos, Amos the father of Josiah. Josiah became the father of Jechoniah and his brothers at the time of the Babylonian exile.

After the Babylonian exile, Jechoniah became the father of Shealtiel, Shealtiel the father of Zerubbabel, Zerubbabel the father of Abiud. Abiud became the father of Eliakim, Eliakim the father of Azor, Azor the father of Zadok. Zadok became the father of Achim, Achim the father of Eliud, Eliud the father of Eleazar. Eleazar became the father of Matthan, Matthan the father of Jacob, Jacob the father of Joseph, the husband of Mary. Of her was born Jesus who is called the Christ.

Thus the total number of generations from Abraham to David is fourteen generations; from David to the Babylonian exile, fourteen generations; from the Babylonian exile to the Christ, fourteen generations.

Now this is how the birth of Jesus Christ came about. When his mother Mary was betrothed to Joseph, but before they lived together, she was found with child through the Holy Spirit. Joseph her husband, since he was a righteous man, yet unwilling to expose her to shame, decided to divorce her quietly. Such was his intention when, behold, the angel of the Lord appeared to him in a dream and said, "Joseph, son of David, do not be afraid to take Mary your wife into your home. For it is through the

Holy Spirit that this child has been conceived in her. She will bear a son and you are to name him Jesus, because he will save his people from their sins." All this took place to fulfill what the Lord had said through the prophet:

Behold, the virgin shall conceive and bear a son,
and they shall name him Emmanuel,

which means "God is with us." When Joseph awoke, he did as the angel of the Lord had commanded him and took his wife into his home. He had no relations with her until she bore a son, and he named him Jesus.

First Reading (Isa 62:1-5)

For Zion's sake I will not be silent,
    for Jerusalem's sake I will not be quiet,
until her vindication shines forth like the dawn
    and her victory like a burning torch.

Nations shall behold your vindication,
    and all the kings your glory;
you shall be called by a new name
    pronounced by the mouth of the LORD.
You shall be a glorious crown in the hand of the LORD,
    a royal diadem held by your God.
No more shall people call you "Forsaken,"
    or your land "Desolate,"
but you shall be called "My Delight,"
    and your land "Espoused."
For the LORD delights in you
    and makes your land his spouse.
As a young man marries a virgin,
    your Builder shall marry you;
and as a bridegroom rejoices in his bride
    so shall your God rejoice in you.

Responsorial Psalm (Ps 89:4-5, 16-17, 27, 29)

℟. (2a) For ever I will sing the goodness of the Lord.

I have made a covenant with my chosen one,
    I have sworn to David my servant:

forever will I confirm your posterity
   and establish your throne for all generations.

R̸. For ever I will sing the goodness of the Lord.

Blessed the people who know the joyful shout;
   in the light of your countenance, O LORD, they walk.
At your name they rejoice all the day,
   and through your justice they are exalted.

R̸. For ever I will sing the goodness of the Lord.

He shall say of me, "You are my father,
   my God, the Rock, my savior."
Forever I will maintain my kindness toward him,
   and my covenant with him stands firm.

R̸. For ever I will sing the goodness of the Lord.

See Appendix, p. 208, for Second Reading

Reflecting on Living the Gospel

God's love is boundless. God's love is intimate. God's love is life-giving salvation. Christmas is truly a feast of love and espoused relationship. God espouses us, and we enter into an intimate relationship with our divine Creator and Lord. The marvelous mystery of the "birth of Jesus Christ came about" because of the marvelous mystery of God's love.

Connecting the Responsorial Psalm to the Readings

In the first reading for the Christmas Vigil Mass God promises to keep acting until salvation is completed. In the second reading Paul expounds how God has relentlessly acted throughout history for this salvation. With its lengthy genealogy the gospel grounds progress toward salvation in real human history, among real human beings. Although this salvation has been long in coming, its coming has been nonetheless certain thanks to the promise of God given in covenant fidelity (responsorial psalm) and spousal love (first reading). As we anticipate tomorrow the full celebration of the birth of Christ we stand with generations who looked forward to this day. May we with them and with Mary and Joseph perceive in ordinary human events the in-breaking of divine miracle. May we stand with them among the blessed who see and sing of "the goodness of the Lord."

Psalmist Preparation

In this responsorial psalm you sing of the covenant made by God with "my chosen one." Do you recognize yourself as "chosen" by God, as participating in the covenant God made with Israel, David, Mary and Joseph? Do you recognize the assembly as "chosen"? How might this awareness affect your singing of this psalm and your celebration of Christmas?

Prayer

God of salvation, in the fullness of time you sent your Son to be with us in human flesh. May we live always as your children, faithful to your covenant and singing of your goodness. We ask this in his name, our Savior and Brother. Amen.

DECEMBER 25, 2015

Gospel (Luke 2:1-14; L14ABC)

In those days a decree went out from Caesar
Augustus that the whole world should be enrolled.
This was the first enrollment, when Quirinius was
governor of Syria. So all went to be enrolled, each to his
own town. And Joseph too went up from Galilee from the
town of Nazareth to Judea, to the city of David that is
called Bethlehem, because he was of the house and
family of David, to be enrolled with Mary, his betrothed, who was with child. While they were there,
the time came for her to have her child, and she gave
birth to her firstborn son. She wrapped him in swaddling clothes and laid him in a manger, because there
was no room for them in the inn.

Now there were shepherds in that region living in the fields and keeping the night watch over their flock. The angel of the Lord appeared to
them and the glory of the Lord shone around them, and they were struck
with great fear. The angel said to them, "Do not be afraid; for behold,
I proclaim to you good news of great joy that will be for all the people. For
today in the city of David a savior has been born for you who is Christ
and Lord. And this will be a sign for you: you will find an infant wrapped
in swaddling clothes and lying in a manger." And suddenly there was a
multitude of the heavenly host with the angel, praising God and saying:

"Glory to God in the highest
    and on earth peace to those on whom his favor rests."

First Reading (Isa 9:1-6)

The people who walked in darkness
    have seen a great light;
upon those who dwelt in the land of gloom
    a light has shone.
You have brought them abundant joy
    and great rejoicing,
as they rejoice before you as at the harvest,
    as people make merry when dividing spoils.
For the yoke that burdened them,
    the pole on their shoulder,

and the rod of their taskmaster
you have smashed, as on the day of Midian.
For every boot that tramped in battle,
every cloak rolled in blood,
will be burned as fuel for flames.
For a child is born to us, a son is given us;
upon his shoulder dominion rests.
They name him Wonder-Counselor, God-Hero,
Father-Forever, Prince of Peace.
His dominion is vast
and forever peaceful,
from David's throne, and over his kingdom,
which he confirms and sustains
by judgment and justice,
both now and forever.
The zeal of the Lord of hosts will do this!

Responsorial Psalm (Ps 96:1-2, 2-3, 11-12, 13)

R℣. (Luke 2:11) Today is born our Savior, Christ the Lord.

Sing to the Lord a new song;
sing to the Lord, all you lands.
Sing to the Lord; bless his name.

R℣. Today is born our Savior, Christ the Lord.

Announce his salvation, day after day.
Tell his glory among the nations;
among all peoples, his wondrous deeds.

R℣. Today is born our Savior, Christ the Lord.

Let the heavens be glad and the earth rejoice;
let the sea and what fills it resound;
let the plains be joyful and all that is in them!
Then shall all the trees of the forest exult.

R℣. Today is born our Savior, Christ the Lord.

They shall exult before the Lord, for he comes;
for he comes to rule the earth.
He shall rule the world with justice
and the peoples with his constancy.

R℣. Today is born our Savior, Christ the Lord.

See Appendix, p. 208, for Second Reading

Reflecting on Living the Gospel

Mary, the virgin, was about to give birth. But she was not alone, not without a loving husband. "Joseph too went up." In this moment of life ushering forth, they shared the intimate love of those who were betrothed. Their shared love would protect, nourish, and teach this divine-human Son.

Connecting the Responsorial Psalm to the Readings

To us human beings who dwell in darkness, burdened and bloodied, the Savior comes (first reading). He comes not in awe and majesty, but born in the night and laid in a manger (gospel). He comes bringing peace, judgment, and justice. He comes to cleanse us so that we be "eager to do what is good" (second reading). The readings for the Mass at Midnight tell us that Christ takes us as we are and enables us to become much more. And so on this most holy night we join the heavens, the seas, even the trees of the forests in rejoicing, for our Savior has been born, and nothing is the same!

Psalmist Preparation

As you prepare to sing this responsorial psalm, use the refrain for daily personal prayer. Let joy and gratitude for the gift of the incarnation fill your heart so that what is in your heart may flow out of your voice when you sing this psalm during the liturgy.

Prayer

God of salvation, you sent your Son to show us light in darkness, hope in hardship, and majesty in littleness. As he took on our humanity, raise us to take on his divinity. We ask this through Christ our Lord. Amen.

Gospel (Luke 2:15-20; L15ABC)

When the angels went away from them to heaven, the shepherds said to one another, "Let us go, then, to Bethlehem to see this thing that has taken place, which the Lord has made known to us." So they went in haste and found Mary and Joseph, and the infant lying in the manger. When they saw this, they made known the message that had been told them about this child. All who heard it were amazed by what had been told them by the shepherds. And Mary kept all these things, reflecting on them in her heart. Then the shepherds returned, glorifying and praising God for all they had heard and seen, just as it had been told to them.

First Reading (Isa 62:11-12)

See, the LORD proclaims
 to the ends of the earth:
say to daughter Zion,
 your savior comes!
Here is his reward with him,
 his recompense before him.
They shall be called the holy people,
 the redeemed of the LORD,
and you shall be called "Frequented,"
 a city that is not forsaken.

Responsorial Psalm (Ps 97:1, 6, 11-12)

R̸. A light will shine on us this day: the Lord is born for us.

The LORD is king; let the earth rejoice;
 let the many isles be glad.
The heavens proclaim his justice,
 and all peoples see his glory.

R̸. A light will shine on us this day: the Lord is born for us.

Light dawns for the just;
 and gladness, for the upright of heart.
Be glad in the LORD, you just,
 and give thanks to his holy name.

R̸. A light will shine on us this day: the Lord is born for us.

See Appendix, p. 208, for Second Reading

Reflecting on Living the Gospel

Every love encounter changes both the lover and the beloved. Our love encounter with this "infant lying in a manger" changes us in the most profound way possible. It saves us. It makes us holy. It makes us heirs of eternal Life.

Connecting the Responsorial Psalm to the Readings

Psalm 97 is one of a set of songs (Psalms 93; 95–100) celebrating God's kingship over other gods, the forces of nature, and the movements of history. For the cultures of the ancient Near East a god was powerful because of some concrete mighty act. In Psalm 97 God manifests the divine Self in clouds, fire, and lightning, making the earth tremble and mountains melt. While those who worship other gods bend in shame, Israel rejoices and sings God's praises.

The few lines from Psalm 97 chosen for the Mass at Dawn fit the calm and quiet of early morning. The angels singing the midnight theophany of God's glory have dispersed. Now we and the simple shepherds tiptoe to the stable to see what we have been told about, the mighty act of God "lying in a manger" (gospel), "born for us" (psalm refrain) in human flesh.

Psalmist Preparation

What "light" dawns today? For whom? How does your singing this morning participate in this light?

Prayer

God of salvation, today your light dawns upon us in the face of your Son come to us in human flesh. May we, like the simple shepherds, tell about this Child to all the world. We ask this in his name. Amen.

THE NATIVITY OF THE LORD
Mass During the Day

Gospel (John 1:1-18 [or John 1:1-5, 9-14]; L16ABC)

In the beginning was the Word,
  and the Word was with God,
  and the Word was God.
He was in the beginning with God.
All things came to be through him,
  and without him nothing came to be.
What came to be through him was life,
  and this life was the light of the
    human race;
the light shines in the darkness,
  and the darkness has not overcome it.

A man named John was sent from God. He came for testimony, to testify to the light, so that all might believe through him. He was not the light, but came to testify to the light. The true light, which enlightens everyone, was coming into the world.

He was in the world,
  and the world came to be through him,
  but the world did not know him.
He came to what was his own,
  but his own people did not accept him.

But to those who did accept him he gave power to become children of God, to those who believe in his name, who were born not by natural generation nor by human choice nor by a man's decision but of God.

And the Word became flesh
  and made his dwelling among us,
  and we saw his glory,
  the glory as of the Father's only Son,
  full of grace and truth.

John testified to him and cried out, saying, "This was he of whom I said, 'The one who is coming after me ranks ahead of me because he existed before me.'" From his fullness we have all received, grace in place of grace, because while the law was given through Moses, grace and truth came through Jesus Christ. No one has ever seen God. The only Son, God, who is at the Father's side, has revealed him.

First Reading (Isa 52:7-10)

How beautiful upon the mountains
    are the feet of him who brings glad tidings,
announcing peace, bearing good news,
    announcing salvation, and saying to Zion,
    "Your God is King!"

Hark! Your sentinels raise a cry,
    together they shout for joy,
for they see directly, before their eyes,
    the LORD restoring Zion.
Break out together in song,
    O ruins of Jerusalem!
For the LORD comforts his people,
    he redeems Jerusalem.
The LORD has bared his holy arm
    in the sight of all the nations;
all the ends of the earth will behold
    the salvation of our God.

Responsorial Psalm (Ps 98:1, 2-3, 3-4, 5-6)

R℣. (3c) All the ends of the earth have seen the saving power of God.

Sing to the LORD a new song,
    for he has done wondrous deeds;
his right hand has won victory for him,
    his holy arm.

R℣. All the ends of the earth have seen the saving power of God.

The LORD has made his salvation known:
    in the sight of the nations he has revealed his justice.
He has remembered his kindness and his faithfulness
    toward the house of Israel.

R℣. All the ends of the earth have seen the saving power of God.

All the ends of the earth have seen
    the salvation by our God.
Sing joyfully to the LORD, all you lands;
    break into song; sing praise.

R℣. All the ends of the earth have seen the saving power of God.

Sing praise to the LORD with the harp,
  with the harp and melodious song.
With trumpets and the sound of the horn
  sing joyfully before the King, the LORD.

℞. All the ends of the earth have seen the saving power of God.

See Appendix, p. 209, for Second Reading

Reflecting on Living the Gospel

In spite of our choosing sometimes to say no to God's overtures of love, of choosing to dwell in darkness instead of the light, the Son of God came to dwell among us, to bring us the fullness of Life, to teach us the kind of self-giving that truly is love made visible.

Connecting the Responsorial Psalm to the Readings

Psalm 98 is an enthronement psalm celebrating God's sovereignty over all creation and all nations. It uses three typical images (God as king, God as warrior, and God as wielder of power), which can be unsettling if we interpret them only on the literal level of Israel's victory in battle over a political enemy. But when we look deeper into the imagery—and into the core of Israel's faith—we discover a God working tirelessly to transform the order of the world so that the lowly may be uplifted and the righteous blessed. This is a God exercising power to corral the wicked, destroy evil, erase suffering, and end oppression. Such is the good news we bear (first reading). But there is more. The gospel announces that through Christ we share in this transforming power. The whole world can sing about the saving power of God because it sees that power working in and through us.

Psalmist Preparation

You call the assembly not only to sing about the saving power of God revealed in the birth of Jesus but to show that power to the world by the manner in which they live. How might you grow in your own confidence in this power of God within you?

Prayer

God of salvation, you sent your Word Jesus to dwell among us so that through him we might become your children. Lead us always to live as your daughters and sons who speak only your Word and spread only your Light. We ask this in his name. Amen.

DECEMBER 27, 2015

Gospel (Luke 2:41-52; L17C)

Each year Jesus' parents went to Jerusalem for the feast of Passover, and when he was twelve years old, they went up according to festival custom. After they had completed its days, as they were returning, the boy Jesus remained behind in Jerusalem, but his parents did not know it. Thinking that he was in the caravan, they journeyed for a day and looked for him among their relatives and acquaintances, but not finding him, they returned to Jerusalem to look for him. After three days they found him in the temple, sitting in the midst of the teachers, listening to them and asking them questions, and all who heard him were astounded at his understanding and his answers. When his parents saw him, they were astonished, and his mother said to him, "Son, why have you done this to us? Your father and I have been looking for you with great anxiety." And he said to them, "Why were you looking for me? Did you not know that I must be in my Father's house?" But they did not understand what he said to them. He went down with them and came to Nazareth, and was obedient to them; and his mother kept all these things in her heart. And Jesus advanced in wisdom and age and favor before God and man.

First Reading (1 Sam 1:20-22, 24-28 [or Sirach 3:2-6, 12-14])

In those days Hannah conceived, and at the end of her term bore a son whom she called Samuel, since she had asked the LORD for him. The next time her husband Elkanah was going up with the rest of his household to offer the customary sacrifice to the LORD and to fulfill his vows, Hannah did not go, explaining to her husband, "Once the child is weaned, I will take him to appear before the LORD and to remain there forever; I will offer him as a perpetual nazirite."

Once Samuel was weaned, Hannah brought him up with her, along with a three-year-old bull, an ephah of flour, and a skin of wine, and presented him at the temple of the LORD in Shiloh. After the boy's father had sacrificed the young bull, Hannah, his mother, approached Eli and said: "Pardon, my lord! As you live, my lord, I am the woman who stood near you here, praying to the LORD. I prayed for this child, and the LORD granted my request. Now I, in turn, give him to the LORD; as long as he lives, he shall be dedicated to the LORD." Hannah left Samuel there.

Responsorial Psalm (Ps 84:2-3, 5-6, 9-10 [or Ps 128:1-2, 3, 4-5])

℟. (cf. 5a) Blessed are they who dwell in your house, O Lord.

How lovely is your dwelling place, O LORD of hosts!
My soul yearns and pines for the courts of the LORD.
My heart and my flesh cry out for the living God.

℟. Blessed are they who dwell in your house, O Lord.

Happy they who dwell in your house!
Continually they praise you.
Happy the men whose strength you are!
Their hearts are set upon the pilgrimage.

℟. Blessed are they who dwell in your house, O Lord.

O LORD of hosts, hear our prayer;
hearken, O God of Jacob!
O God, behold our shield,
and look upon the face of your anointed.

℟. Blessed are they who dwell in your house, O Lord.

See Appendix, p. 209, for Second Reading

Reflecting on Living the Gospel

So much tradition shapes the event in this gospel: Passover in Jerusalem, significance of being twelve years old, traveling in caravan, being in the temple, obedience to parents. A surprising interruption of tradition also shapes this event: "the boy Jesus" astounded the teachers "at his understanding and his answers." Each family—the Holy Family, our own families—must find a way to keep worthy traditions alive while at the same time remain open to something astoundingly new. Holiness consists in finding that way.

Connecting the Responsorial Psalm to the Readings

For the Israelites God's dwelling place was the temple in Jerusalem. There they journeyed three times a year to keep festival. These annual pilgrimages were joyous occasions, expressing the community's sense of identity as God's chosen people and their longing to be with God forever. Psalm 84 communicates this joy and this hope.

Because she knew she was one of God's chosen people, Hannah willingly gave her son to God (first reading). Because he knew he was God's

Son, Jesus recognized his "Father's house" as his true home (gospel). We, too, know who we are—"the children of God"—and where we dwell— "in him" (second reading). Like Jesus, like Mary and Joseph, like Hannah, we give ourselves in obedience and trust to the God who has made us God's own. We sing Psalm 84 to celebrate *our* blessedness as God's chosen ones and to express our desire to dwell more fully in God's presence.

Psalmist Preparation

In this responsorial psalm you call the assembly to become conscious of who they are—a holy family who dwells in the house of the Lord. What would strengthen your own sense of yourself as a member of God's family? How might you live this week so that this identity be more evident to others?

Prayer

God of heaven and earth, you call us together as family and invite us to dwell with you in holiness. Keep us always faithful to your covenant and reverent toward one another. We ask this through Christ our Lord. Amen.

Gospel (Luke 2:16-21; L18ABC)

The shepherds went in haste to Bethlehem and found Mary and Joseph, and the infant lying in the manger. When they saw this, they made known the message that had been told them about this child. All who heard it were amazed by what had been told them by the shepherds. And Mary kept all these things, reflecting on them in her heart. Then the shepherds returned, glorifying and praising God for all they had heard and seen, just as it had been told to them.

When eight days were completed for his circumcision, he was named Jesus, the name given him by the angel before he was conceived in the womb.

First Reading (Num 6:22-27)

The LORD said to Moses: "Speak to Aaron and his sons and tell them: This is how you shall bless the Israelites. Say to them:

The LORD bless you and keep you!
The LORD let his face shine upon you, and be gracious to you!
The LORD look upon you kindly and give you peace!

So shall they invoke my name upon the Israelites, and I will bless them."

Responsorial Psalm (Ps 67:2-3, 5, 6, 8)

R℣. (2a) May God bless us in his mercy.

May God have pity on us and bless us;
    may he let his face shine upon us.
So may your way be known upon earth;
    among all nations, your salvation.

R℣. May God bless us in his mercy.

May the nations be glad and exult
    because you rule the peoples in equity;
    the nations on the earth you guide.

R℣. May God bless us in his mercy.

May the peoples praise you, O God;
  may all the peoples praise you!
May God bless us,
  and may all the ends of the earth fear him!

R̼. May God bless us in his mercy.

See Appendix, p. 209, for Second Reading

Reflecting on Living the Gospel

The shepherds obeyed the angel's revelation and searched for the new-born babe, the Savior, the Messiah. Mary, the Mother of this wondrous Child, also had a message made known to her by an angel. She heard, accepted, and said yes to what God revealed to her. She is the Mother of God. She is our Mother who helps us hear this same message. When do we go "in haste," like the shepherds, and tell everyone we meet what has been told to us?

Connecting the Responsorial Psalm to the Readings

The Lectionary omits the verse from Psalm 67 that marks it as a song of thanksgiving for a bountiful harvest: "The earth has yielded its harvest; / God, our God, blesses us" (v. 7). In singing Psalm 67 the Israelites not only thanked God for all that had been given to them but also asked God to extend this bounty to all peoples. On this solemnity we celebrate that the mercy of God has caused the earthly flesh of Mary to yield its greatest blessing, the body of Jesus (gospel). It is through this blessing that we are harvested as God's own children (second reading). In singing Psalm 67 we acknowledge the unimaginable magnitude of God's mercy toward us, and we pray that all peoples come to know their blessedness in Christ.

Psalmist Preparation

As you prepare to sing this responsorial psalm, reflect on how blessed you are because of the birth of Christ. Do you realize that you are a child of God? Do you know how favored you are? Coming to see who you are because of Christ will enable you to pray that all people may come to know this same blessedness.

Prayer

Saving God, you brought the mystery of salvation to fulfillment in the flesh of Mary. May we, with her, contemplate this wondrous blessing that brings heaven to earth. May we, like her, allow the mystery of your salvation to come to birth in our human flesh. We ask this through Christ our Lord. Amen.

Gospel (Matt 2:1-12; L20ABC)

When Jesus was born in Bethlehem of Judea, in the days of King Herod, behold, magi from the east arrived in Jerusalem, saying, "Where is the newborn king of the Jews? We saw his star at its rising and have come to do him homage." When King Herod heard this, he was greatly troubled, and all Jerusalem with him. Assembling all the chief priests and the scribes of the people, he inquired of them where the Christ was to be born. They said to him, "In Bethlehem of Judea, for thus it has been written through the prophet:

> And you, Bethlehem, land of Judah,
>   are by no means least among the rulers of Judah;
> since from you shall come a ruler,
>   who is to shepherd my people Israel."

Then Herod called the magi secretly and ascertained from them the time of the star's appearance. He sent them to Bethlehem and said, "Go and search diligently for the child. When you have found him, bring me word, that I too may go and do him homage." After their audience with the king they set out. And behold, the star that they had seen at its rising preceded them, until it came and stopped over the place where the child was. They were overjoyed at seeing the star, and on entering the house they saw the child with Mary his mother. They prostrated themselves and did him homage. Then they opened their treasures and offered him gifts of gold, frankincense, and myrrh. And having been warned in a dream not to return to Herod, they departed for their country by another way.

First Reading (Isa 60:1-6)

Rise up in splendor, Jerusalem! Your light has come,
  the glory of the Lord shines upon you.
See, darkness covers the earth,
  and thick clouds cover the peoples;
but upon you the Lord shines,
  and over you appears his glory.
Nations shall walk by your light,
  and kings by your shining radiance.

Raise your eyes and look about;
  they all gather and come to you:
your sons come from afar,
  and your daughters in the arms of their nurses.

Then you shall be radiant at what you see,
  your heart shall throb and overflow,
for the riches of the sea shall be emptied out before you,
  the wealth of nations shall be brought to you.
Caravans of camels shall fill you,
  dromedaries from Midian and Ephah;
all from Sheba shall come
  bearing gold and frankincense,
  and proclaiming the praises of the LORD.

Responsorial Psalm (Ps 72:1-2, 7-8, 10-11, 12-13)

R̸. (cf. 11) Lord, every nation on earth will adore you.

O God, with your judgment endow the king,
  and with your justice, the king's son;
he shall govern your people with justice
  and your afflicted ones with judgment.

R̸. Lord, every nation on earth will adore you.

Justice shall flower in his days,
  and profound peace, till the moon be no more.
May he rule from sea to sea,
  and from the River to the ends of the earth.

R̸. Lord, every nation on earth will adore you.

The kings of Tarshish and the Isles shall offer gifts;
  the kings of Arabia and Seba shall bring tribute.
All kings shall pay him homage,
  all nations shall serve him.

R̸. Lord, every nation on earth will adore you.

For he shall rescue the poor when he cries out,
  and the afflicted when he has no one to help him.
He shall have pity for the lowly and the poor;
  the lives of the poor he shall save.

R̸. Lord, every nation on earth will adore you.

See Appendix, p. 210, for Second Reading

Reflecting on Living the Gospel

The "magi from the east" followed the light of a star. A light of heaven that guided them. A light of revelation that manifested "the newborn king of the Jews" to Gentile wise men. A light of warning that protected this Child from harm until his time had come. Like the magi, we must follow this light to *the* Light. Like the magi, we must offer "the child" homage—the gift of our very selves become the Light of his Presence.

Connecting the Responsorial Psalm to the Readings

Historically, Psalm 72 was a prayer for the king of Israel who represented God. The people asked God to endow the king with divine judgment so that justice might reign, the poor and afflicted be rescued, and peace blossom for all time. Then light would shine from Jerusalem and all nations would recognize and pay homage to the true King, the Lord God (first reading).

Liturgically, the Lectionary uses verses from Psalm 72 to identify Christ as the fulfillment of Israel's prayer: this newborn babe is the King par excellence, God's justice and mercy in the flesh, come to rescue the poor and bring peace to all nations. Those who "see" recognize who he is and come to adore him (gospel). In the second reading, Paul tells us the revelation made known in the coming of Christ is complete and universal. Nonetheless, leading all people to see and recognize Christ requires action on our part: we are "copartners in . . . Christ." And so our singing of this psalm is more than just a celebration of what God has done for salvation. It is also a commitment on our part to spread the Good News of God's saving work to all nations.

Psalmist Preparation

When you sing this responsorial psalm, you reveal who Christ is: the justice, peace, and mercy of God in human flesh. You also participate in the church's prayer that all peoples recognize who Christ is and come to adore him. What might you do this week to be the justice of God in human flesh for someone? Who needs you to be the mercy of God made flesh?

Prayer

Redeemer God, you sent your Son to be salvation for all peoples. Fill us with his Spirit that we may be his justice, his mercy, and his peace in the world so that all may come to know your name and sing your goodness. We ask this in his name. Amen.

43

THE BAPTISM OF THE LORD

Gospel (Luke 3:15-16, 21-22; L21C)

The people were filled with expectation, and all were asking in their hearts whether John might be the Christ. John answered them all, saying, "I am baptizing you with water, but one mightier than I is coming. I am not worthy to loosen the thongs of his sandals. He will baptize you with the Holy Spirit and fire."

After all the people had been baptized and Jesus also had been baptized and was praying, heaven was opened and the Holy Spirit descended upon him in bodily form like a dove. And a voice came from heaven, "You are my beloved Son; with you I am well pleased."

First Reading (Isa 40:1-5, 9-11 [or Isa 42:1-4, 6-7])

Comfort, give comfort to my people,
    says your God.
Speak tenderly to Jerusalem, and proclaim to her
    that her service is at an end,
    her guilt is expiated;
indeed, she has received from the hand of the LORD
    double for all her sins.

    A voice cries out:
In the desert prepare the way of the LORD!
    Make straight in the wasteland a highway for our God!
Every valley shall be filled in,
    every mountain and hill shall be made low;
the rugged land shall be made a plain,
    the rough country, a broad valley.
Then the glory of the LORD shall be revealed,
    and all people shall see it together;
    for the mouth of the LORD has spoken.

Go up onto a high mountain,
    Zion, herald of glad tidings;
cry out at the top of your voice,
    Jerusalem, herald of good news!

Fear not to cry out
　and say to the cities of Judah:
　Here is your God!
Here comes with power
　the Lord GOD,
　who rules by a strong arm;
here is his reward with him,
　his recompense before him.
Like a shepherd he feeds his flock;
　in his arms he gathers the lambs,
carrying them in his bosom,
　and leading the ewes with care.

Responsorial Psalm (Ps 104:1b-2, 3-4, 24-25, 27-28, 29-30 [or Ps 29:1-2, 3-4, 3, 9-10])

℟. (1) O bless the Lord, my soul.

O LORD, my God, you are great indeed!
　You are clothed with majesty and glory,
robed in light as with a cloak.
　You have spread out the heavens like a tent-cloth.

℟. O bless the Lord, my soul.

You have constructed your palace upon the waters.
　You make the clouds your chariot;
you travel on the wings of the wind.
　You make the winds your messengers,
and flaming fire your ministers.

℟. O bless the Lord, my soul.

How manifold are your works, O LORD!
　In wisdom you have wrought them all—
the earth is full of your creatures;
　the sea also, great and wide,
in which are schools without number
　of living things both small and great.

℟. O bless the Lord, my soul.

They look to you to give them food in due time.
    When you give it to them, they gather it;
when you open your hand, they are filled with good things.

R̸. O bless the Lord, my soul.

If you take away their breath, they perish and return to the dust.
    When you send forth your spirit, they are created,
and you renew the face of the earth.

R̸. O bless the Lord, my soul.

See Appendix, p. 210, for Second Reading

Reflecting on Living the Gospel

The people in the gospel looked to John the Baptist to be the long-awaited Messiah. It was precisely their expectation—misdirected though it was—that kept them looking for the Messiah. John redirected them from himself to the person of Jesus, the "beloved Son" of God. Our own baptism with "the Holy Spirit and fire" initiates us on a journey of discovery not only of who Jesus is but also who we are in him: the beloved of God.

Connecting the Responsorial Psalm to the Readings

In these verses from Psalm 104, we praise God who spreads out the heavens, rules the water and the wind, creates all that roams the earth and swims the seas, and gives all creatures their food in due season. The readings and gospel reveal that the fullness of God's power and glory has appeared in the person of Christ. He is God's "beloved Son" (gospel) who will shepherd us to fuller life (see first reading). He is the Son who will "baptize [us] with the Holy Spirit" (gospel), setting us on fire as a people "eager to do . . . good" (second reading). He is the Son through whom the Spirit will "renew the face of the earth" (psalm). Let us cry out at the top of our voices that in him salvation has come, and God is here (see first reading)!

Psalmist Preparation

In these psalm verses, you bless God for giving the Spirit of life, for giving the "beloved Son" who leads us to fullness of Life, for giving the baptism that sets us on fire to "do good." In fact, you sing some of the same psalm verses you will sing later in the liturgical year for Pentecost Sunday. What is the connection between Christ's baptism and Pentecost? between your baptism and Pentecost?

Prayer

Glorious God, you are well pleased in your Son Jesus. Keep us who are baptized into his Body also pleasing to you so that our manner of living may manifest to the world your saving power and grace. We ask this in his name. Amen.

Gospel (John 2:1-11; L66C)

There was a wedding at Cana in Galilee, and the mother of Jesus was there. Jesus and his disciples were also invited to the wedding. When the wine ran short, the mother of Jesus said to him, "They have no wine." And Jesus said to her, "Woman, how does your concern affect me? My hour has not yet come." His mother said to the servers, "Do whatever he tells you." Now there were six stone water jars there for Jewish ceremonial washings, each holding twenty to thirty gallons. Jesus told them, "Fill the jars with water." So they filled them to the brim. Then he told them, "Draw some out now and take it to the headwaiter." So they took it. And when the headwaiter tasted the water that had become wine, without knowing where it came from —although the servers who had drawn the water knew—, the headwaiter called the bridegroom and said to him, "Everyone serves good wine first, and then when people have drunk freely, an inferior one; but you have kept the good wine until now." Jesus did this as the beginning of his signs at Cana in Galilee and so revealed his glory, and his disciples began to believe in him.

First Reading (Isa 62:1-5)

For Zion's sake I will not be silent,
    for Jerusalem's sake I will not be quiet,
until her vindication shines forth like the dawn
    and her victory like a burning torch.

Nations shall behold your vindication,
    and all the kings your glory;
you shall be called by a new name
    pronounced by the mouth of the LORD.
You shall be a glorious crown in the hand of the LORD,
    a royal diadem held by your God.
No more shall people call you "Forsaken,"
    or your land "Desolate,"
but you shall be called "My Delight,"
    and your land "Espoused."
For the LORD delights in you
    and makes your land his spouse.

48

As a young man marries a virgin,
    your Builder shall marry you;
and as a bridegroom rejoices in his bride
    so shall your God rejoice in you.

Responsorial Psalm (Ps 96:1-2, 2-3, 7-8, 9-10)

R⎸. (3) Proclaim his marvelous deeds to all the nations.

Sing to the LORD a new song;
    sing to the LORD, all you lands.
Sing to the LORD; bless his name.

R⎸. Proclaim his marvelous deeds to all the nations.

Announce his salvation, day after day.
Tell his glory among the nations;
    among all peoples, his wondrous deeds.

R⎸. Proclaim his marvelous deeds to all the nations.

Give to the LORD, you families of nations,
    give to the LORD glory and praise;
    give to the LORD the glory due his name!

R⎸. Proclaim his marvelous deeds to all the nations.

Worship the LORD in holy attire.
    Tremble before him, all the earth;
say among the nations: The LORD is king.
    He governs the peoples with equity.

R⎸. Proclaim his marvelous deeds to all the nations.

Second Reading (1 Cor 12:4-11)

Reflecting on Living the Gospel

What is Jesus' "hour"? It is a time of the revelation of God's immense gift of abundance. In this gospel, not one jar of water became wine, but six. Not partially filled jars, but "to the brim." Not inferior wine, but "good wine." Not just one sign, but "the beginning of his signs." God's glory is revealed in many signs of abundance. Most fully in Jesus himself. Most fully in us, the Body of Christ, as we come to deeper belief and continue his ministry.

Connecting the Responsorial Psalm to the Readings

These verses from Psalm 96 begin by commanding us to sing to God, bless God's name, announce God's wondrous deeds to all the world. They conclude with us calling all nations to join in our praise and worship of God. The first reading and gospel reveal that what we praise God for is the superabundance of the gift of salvation. God surpasses the wants and dreams of the Israelites, transforming their identity (first reading). Jesus surpasses the expectations of the wedding guests, transforming ordinary water into extraordinary wine (gospel). Those who saw this sign came to believe in him. In this responsorial psalm we announce that we, too, see in the person of Jesus the superabundance of God's gift of salvation, and we want to tell all the world.

Psalmist Preparation

Sometimes the saving acts of God come in extraordinary ways, but most often they come in the quiet events of ordinary, everyday living. The trick is to see these signs so that you can believe. How is Christ turning the ordinary water of your life into the wine of salvation?

Prayer

All-powerful God, you work marvelous deeds of salvation. Help us to recognize the changes and transformations you continually bring about in our world that we may announce your saving deeds to all nations. We ask this through Christ our Lord. Amen.

Gospel (Luke 1:1-4; 4:14-21; L69C)

Since many have undertaken to compile a narrative of the events that have been fulfilled among us, just as those who were eyewitnesses from the beginning and ministers of the word have handed them down to us, I too have decided, after investigating everything accurately anew, to write it down in an orderly sequence for you, most excellent Theophilus, so that you may realize the certainty of the teachings you have received.

Jesus returned to Galilee in the power of the Spirit, and news of him spread throughout the whole region. He taught in their synagogues and was praised by all.

He came to Nazareth, where he had grown up, and went according to his custom into the synagogue on the sabbath day. He stood up to read and was handed a scroll of the prophet Isaiah. He unrolled the scroll and found the passage where it was written:

> The Spirit of the Lord is upon me,
>   because he has anointed me
>   to bring glad tidings to the poor.
> He has sent me to proclaim liberty to captives
>   and recovery of sight to the blind,
>   to let the oppressed go free,
>   and to proclaim a year acceptable to the Lord.

Rolling up the scroll, he handed it back to the attendant and sat down, and the eyes of all in the synagogue looked intently at him. He said to them, "Today this Scripture passage is fulfilled in your hearing."

First Reading (Neh 8:2-4a, 5-6, 8-10)

Ezra the priest brought the law before the assembly, which consisted of men, women, and those children old enough to understand. Standing at one end of the open place that was before the Water Gate, he read out of the book from daybreak till midday, in the presence of the men, the women, and those children old enough to understand; and all the people listened attentively to the book of the law. Ezra the scribe stood on a wooden platform that had been made for the occasion. He opened the scroll so that all the people might see it—for he was standing higher up than any of the people—; and, as he opened it, all the people rose.

Ezra blessed the LORD, the great God, and all the people, their hands raised high, answered, "Amen, amen!" Then they bowed down and prostrated themselves before the LORD, their faces to the ground. Ezra read plainly from the book of the law of God, interpreting it so that all could understand what was read. Then Nehemiah, that is, His Excellency, and Ezra the priest-scribe and the Levites who were instructing the people said to all the people: "Today is holy to the LORD your God. Do not be sad, and do not weep"—for all the people were weeping as they heard the words of the law. He said further: "Go, eat rich foods and drink sweet drinks, and allot portions to those who had nothing prepared; for today is holy to our LORD. Do not be saddened this day, for rejoicing in the LORD must be your strength!"

Responsorial Psalm (Ps 19:8, 9, 10, 15)

℟. (cf. John 6:63c) Your words, Lord, are Spirit and life.

The law of the LORD is perfect,
    refreshing the soul;
the decree of the LORD is trustworthy,
    giving wisdom to the simple.

℟. Your words, Lord, are Spirit and life.

The precepts of the LORD are right,
    rejoicing the heart;
the command of the LORD is clear,
    enlightening the eye.

℟. Your words, Lord, are Spirit and life.

The fear of the LORD is pure,
    enduring forever;
the ordinances of the LORD are true,
    all of them just.

℟. Your words, Lord, are Spirit and life.

Let the words of my mouth and the thought of my heart
    find favor before you,
O LORD, my rock and my redeemer.

℟. Your words, Lord, are Spirit and life.

Second Reading (1 Cor 12:12-30 [or 1 Cor 12:12-14, 27])

Reflecting on Living the Gospel
In this gospel Jesus clearly proclaims who he is and what he comes to bring. He is One who lives "in the power of the Spirit"; he comes to bring a new teaching. He is God's anointed; he comes to bring the human community glad tidings, liberty, sight, freedom, favor. He is the long-awaited Messiah; he comes to bring manifest signs of salvation. The "eyes of all . . . looked intently at him." Do our own eyes look intently upon him?

Connecting the Responsorial Psalm to the Readings
The responsorial psalm proclaims that the word of God is perfect, trustworthy, right, and clear. The word of God refreshes the soul, rejoices the heart, and enlightens the eye. In the first reading this word is the Law read by Ezra to the assembled people who weep at its hearing. In the gospel this word from the prophet Isaiah is announced by Jesus to the synagogue gathering who "looked intently at him" for its interpretation. His interpretation is a stunner: this word is his very person "fulfilled in your hearing."

The word of God given in the Law and the Prophets expresses God's will for human salvation. Jesus reveals that this will is himself, the Word-will of God in flesh and bone, bringing Good News to the poor, restoring sight to the blind, and granting freedom to the oppressed. The Word which is trustworthy and clear, which rejoices the heart and enlightens the eye, is the very person of Christ. He is the Word/Law about which we sing in Psalm 19.

Psalmist Preparation
The word of God about which you sing in this responsorial psalm is fulfilled in the person of Christ. As you pray the psalm in preparation this week, you might substitute the name of Christ for the words "law," "decree," "precept," and so on. How does this deepen your understanding of who Christ is? How will this affect your singing of the psalm?

Prayer
Giver of truth and life, you send your Word to guide us along the path of salvation. Keep us faithful to this Word in our every thought and action that we may be Jesus' saving presence for all whom we meet. We ask this in his name. Amen.

Gospel (Luke 4:21-30; L72C)

Jesus began speaking in the synagogue, saying: "Today this Scripture passage is fulfilled in your hearing." And all spoke highly of him and were amazed at the gracious words that came from his mouth. They also asked, "Isn't this the son of Joseph?" He said to them, "Surely you will quote me this proverb, 'Physician, cure yourself,' and say, 'Do here in your native place the things that we heard were done in Capernaum.'" And he said, "Amen, I say to you, no prophet is accepted in his own native place. Indeed, I tell you, there were many widows in Israel in the days of Elijah when the sky was closed for three and a half years and a severe famine spread over the entire land. It was to none of these that Elijah was sent, but only to a widow in Zarephath in the land of Sidon. Again, there were many lepers in Israel during the time of Elisha the prophet; yet not one of them was cleansed, but only Naaman the Syrian." When the people in the synagogue heard this, they were all filled with fury. They rose up, drove him out of the town, and led him to the brow of the hill on which their town had been built, to hurl him down headlong. But Jesus passed through the midst of them and went away.

First Reading (Jer 1:4-5, 17-19)

The word of the LORD came to me, saying:

Before I formed you in the womb I knew you,
    before you were born I dedicated you,
    a prophet to the nations I appointed you.

But do you gird your loins;
    stand up and tell them
    all that I command you.
Be not crushed on their account,
    as though I would leave you crushed before them;
for it is I this day
    who have made you a fortified city,
a pillar of iron, a wall of brass,
    against the whole land:

against Judah's kings and princes,
    against its priests and people.
They will fight against you but not prevail over you,
    for I am with you to deliver you, says the LORD.

Responsorial Psalm (Ps 71:1-2, 3-4, 5-6, 15, 17)

℟. (cf. 15ab) I will sing of your salvation.

In you, O LORD, I take refuge;
    let me never be put to shame.
In your justice rescue me, and deliver me;
    incline your ear to me, and save me.

℟. I will sing of your salvation.

Be my rock of refuge,
    a stronghold to give me safety,
    for you are my rock and my fortress.
O my God, rescue me from the hand of the wicked.

℟. I will sing of your salvation.

For you are my hope, O Lord;
    my trust, O God, from my youth.
On you I depend from birth;
    from my mother's womb you are my strength.

℟. I will sing of your salvation.

My mouth shall declare your justice,
    day by day your salvation.
O God, you have taught me from my youth,
    and till the present I proclaim your wondrous deeds.

℟. I will sing of your salvation.

Second Reading (1 Cor 13:4-13 [or 1 Cor 12:31–13:13])

Reflecting on Living the Gospel

More than one Scripture passage is being fulfilled in this gospel. The
words and deeds of Jesus fulfill the Scripture passage from Isaiah about
the coming of salvation: glad tidings for the poor, liberty for captives,
sight for the blind, freedom for the oppressed. The words and deeds of
the people fulfill the Scripture passages about rejecting and killing God's

prophets: they question Jesus' origins, become furious at his words, and act to destroy him. Which Scripture passages do we hear?

Connecting the Responsorial Psalm to the Readings

Like Jesus (gospel) and Jeremiah (first reading), we are sent to proclaim salvation to the world. Like Jesus and Jeremiah, we will meet opposition, persecution, even death as we fulfill this mission. But the psalm promises we shall be protected even as we are persecuted, for the God who has loved us since before our birth will be our salvation. The psalm invites us to fulfill our mission fully conscious of the suffering it will bring, but equally conscious of the salvation God has promised beyond that suffering. This is not a psalm that we sing naively, but with hope-filled realism. And Jesus sings with us.

Psalmist Preparation

The confidence expressed in this psalm counterbalances the reality of persecution faced by those who remain faithful to God's call (first reading, gospel). If you choose to be faithful to the mission you share with Christ, you will meet opposition and rejection. But you will also have the presence and protection of God who will be leading you to Life. Do you believe this? Are you willing to make the same choice as Jesus?

Prayer

Loving God, you protect those who stake their lives on your word. Keep us faithful to your word, courageous in discipleship, and constant in singing of your salvation. We ask this through Christ our Lord. Amen.

Gospel (Luke 5:1-11; L75C)

While the crowd was pressing in on Jesus and listening to the word of God, he was standing by the Lake of Gennesaret. He saw two boats there alongside the lake; the fishermen had disembarked and were washing their nets. Getting into one of the boats, the one belonging to Simon, he asked him to put out a short distance from the shore. Then he sat down and taught the crowds from the boat. After he had finished speaking, he said to Simon, "Put out into deep water and lower your nets for a catch." Simon said in reply, "Master, we have worked hard all night and have caught nothing, but at your command I will lower the nets." When they had done this, they caught a great number of fish and their nets were tearing. They signaled to their partners in the other boat to come to help them. They came and filled both boats so that the boats were in danger of sinking. When Simon Peter saw this, he fell at the knees of Jesus and said, "Depart from me, Lord, for I am a sinful man." For astonishment at the catch of fish they had made seized him and all those with him, and likewise James and John, the sons of Zebedee, who were partners of Simon. Jesus said to Simon, "Do not be afraid; from now on you will be catching men." When they brought their boats to the shore, they left everything and followed him.

First Reading (Isa 6:1-2a, 3-8)

In the year King Uzziah died, I saw the Lord seated on a high and lofty throne, with the train of his garment filling the temple. Seraphim were stationed above.

They cried one to the other, "Holy, holy, holy is the LORD of hosts! All the earth is filled with his glory!" At the sound of that cry, the frame of the door shook and the house was filled with smoke.

Then I said, "Woe is me, I am doomed! For I am a man of unclean lips, living among a people of unclean lips; yet my eyes have seen the King, the LORD of hosts!" Then one of the seraphim flew to me, holding an ember that he had taken with tongs from the altar.

He touched my mouth with it, and said, "See, now that this has touched your lips, your wickedness is removed, your sin purged."

57

Then I heard the voice of the Lord saying, "Whom shall I send? Who will go for us?" "Here I am," I said; "send me!"

Responsorial Psalm (Ps 138:1-2, 2-3, 4-5, 7-8)

R℣. (1c) In the sight of the angels I will sing your praises, Lord.

I will give thanks to you, O LORD, with all my heart,
    for you have heard the words of my mouth;
    in the presence of the angels I will sing your praise;
I will worship at your holy temple
    and give thanks to your name.

R℣. In the sight of the angels I will sing your praises, Lord.

Because of your kindness and your truth;
    for you have made great above all things
    your name and your promise.
When I called, you answered me;
    you built up strength within me.

R℣. In the sight of the angels I will sing your praises, Lord.

All the kings of the earth shall give thanks to you, O LORD,
    when they hear the words of your mouth;
and they shall sing of the ways of the LORD:
    "Great is the glory of the LORD."

R℣. In the sight of the angels I will sing your praises, Lord.

Your right hand saves me.
    The LORD will complete what he has done for me;
your kindness, O LORD, endures forever;
    forsake not the work of your hands.

R℣. In the sight of the angels I will sing your praises, Lord.

Second Reading (1 Cor 15:3-8, 11 [or 1 Cor 15:1-11])

Reflecting on Living the Gospel
After fishing all night and catching nothing, Peter obeys Jesus, putting out his boat and nets once again. He makes a great catch of fish. Even more, he comes to a great insight about himself. Encounter with Jesus leads Peter to see himself as he really is ("I am a sinful man"), and to become what he is not yet: a follower of Jesus participating in his saving mission. Jesus "caught" Peter. He will "catch" us, too. Will he?

Connecting the Responsorial Psalm to the Readings

Encounter with the Holy One, be it the "LORD of hosts" in heaven (first reading) or Jesus in an ordinary life situation (gospel), is a wake-up call. Individuals are shaken out of their complacency and change the direction of their lives. Both Isaiah and Peter acknowledge their own unholiness, and then find themselves sent on mission. The responsorial psalm reveals more beneath the surface, however. God heard the "words" uttered by Isaiah and Peter. God perceived the weakness each felt and replaced it with strength. Supported by such divine initiative, these two readily accept their mission, for they are confident that God "will complete what he has" begun in them.

The Holy One comes to us, too, sometimes in extraordinary ways, but most times in the ordinary circumstances of our daily lives. Each time, the Holy One shows us ourselves as we really are, strengthens us, then sends us to continue our baptismal mission. Like Isaiah and Peter we can readily respond, "Send me!" for we know, as does the psalmist, who has begun and who will complete this work in us.

Psalmist Preparation

What is the mission to which God calls you as psalmist? To what extent do you feel unworthy of this mission? How does God give you the confidence and strength you need? And how is this mission changing your life?

Prayer

God of power and majesty, you confront us with truth and confirm us for mission. Cleanse us of all that impedes the work of your grace within us that we may proclaim your saving deeds to all creatures in heaven and on earth. We ask this through Christ our Lord. Amen.

Gospel (Matt 6:1-6, 16-18; L219)

Jesus said to his disciples: "Take care not to perform righteous deeds in order that people may see them; otherwise, you will have no recompense from your heavenly Father. When you give alms, do not blow a trumpet before you, as the hypocrites do in the synagogues and in the streets to win the praise of others. Amen, I say to you, they have received their reward. But when you give alms, do not let your left hand know what your right is doing, so that your almsgiving may be secret. And your Father who sees in secret will repay you.

"When you pray, do not be like the hypocrites, who love to stand and pray in the synagogues and on street corners so that others may see them. Amen, I say to you, they have received their reward. But when you pray, go to your inner room, close the door, and pray to your Father in secret. And your Father who sees in secret will repay you.

"When you fast, do not look gloomy like the hypocrites. They neglect their appearance, so that they may appear to others to be fasting. Amen, I say to you, they have received their reward. But when you fast, anoint your head and wash your face, so that you may not appear to be fasting, except to your Father who is hidden. And your Father who sees what is hidden will repay you."

First Reading (Joel 2:12-18)

Even now, says the LORD,
 return to me with your whole heart,
 with fasting, and weeping, and mourning;
Rend your hearts, not your garments,
 and return to the LORD, your God.
For gracious and merciful is he,
 slow to anger, rich in kindness,
 and relenting in punishment.
Perhaps he will again relent
 and leave behind him a blessing,
Offerings and libations
 for the LORD, your God.

Blow the trumpet in Zion!
  proclaim a fast,
  call an assembly;
Gather the people,
  notify the congregation;
Assemble the elders,
  gather the children
  and the infants at the breast;
Let the bridegroom quit his room
  and the bride her chamber.
Between the porch and the altar
  let the priests, the ministers of the LORD, weep,
And say, "Spare, O LORD, your people,
  and make not your heritage a reproach,
  with the nations ruling over them!
Why should they say among the peoples,
  'Where is their God?'"

Then the LORD was stirred to concern for his land and took pity on his people.

Responsorial Psalm (Ps 51:3-4, 5-6ab, 12-13, 14, and 17)

℟. (see 3a) Be merciful, O Lord, for we have sinned.

Have mercy on me, O God, in your goodness;
  in the greatness of your compassion wipe out my offense.
Thoroughly wash me from my guilt
  and of my sin cleanse me.

℟. Be merciful, O Lord, for we have sinned.

For I acknowledge my offense,
  and my sin is before me always:
"Against you only have I sinned,
  and done what is evil in your sight."

℟. Be merciful, O Lord, for we have sinned.

A clean heart create for me, O God,
  and a steadfast spirit renew within me.
Cast me not out from your presence,
  and your Holy Spirit take not from me.

℟. Be merciful, O Lord, for we have sinned.

Give me back the joy of your salvation,
and a willing spirit sustain in me.
O Lord, open my lips,
and my mouth shall proclaim your praise.

R̷. Be merciful, O Lord, for we have sinned.

See Appendix, p. 210, for Second Reading

Reflecting on Living the Gospel

The spirit in which we do penance—and, indeed, the purpose of all of
Lent—is openness to *God's work* in us leading to conversion of heart.
Lenten penance that transforms us and makes a difference in our on-
going daily living and deepens our relationship with God and each other
is our response to God's overture of Presence and grace. The outward
signs of Lenten penance are indications that God is at work in us. Even
our choice to do penance is a response to God.

Connecting the Responsorial Psalm to the Readings

As we do every year, we begin our annual season of penance and transformation by singing Psalm 51. Of all the penitential psalms, Psalm 51 is
the most open in its confession of sin and the most poignant in its plea
for God's mercy. Psalm 51 takes us to that "secret" place (gospel) where
we "rend our hearts" (first reading) so that God may change them (psalm).
The good news is that God will do the cleansing work of transforming
our inner selves (psalm). We have only to open our hearts and ask.

Psalmist Preparation

In singing Psalm 51 you acknowledge that you have not always been
faithful and ask God to bring you back by re-creating your heart. You
stand before the assembly as a living embodiment of both sides of the
story of salvation: human sinfulness and divine mercy. Such witness demands a great deal of honesty and vulnerability. What can help you be
honest before God? What can help you be vulnerable before the
community?

Prayer

God of compassion, you embrace in mercy the sinner who returns to you
with a contrite heart. Lead us through our Lenten practices of prayer,
penance, and almsgiving to turn our hearts more fully toward you that
we may rise transformed with new life on Easter. We ask this through
Christ our Lord. Amen.

Gospel (Luke 4:1-13; L24C)

Filled with the Holy Spirit, Jesus returned
from the Jordan and was led by the
Spirit into the desert for forty days, to
be tempted by the devil. He ate nothing
during those days, and when they were
over he was hungry. The devil said to him,
"If you are the Son of God, command this
stone to become bread." Jesus answered him,
"It is written, *One does not live on bread
alone.*" Then he took him up and showed him all
the kingdoms of the world in a single instant. The devil said to him, "I
shall give to you all this power and glory; for it has been handed over to
me, and I may give it to whomever I wish. All this will be yours, if you
worship me." Jesus said to him in reply, "It is written:

> *You shall worship the Lord, your God,*
> *and him alone shall you serve."*

Then he led him to Jerusalem, made him stand on the parapet of the
temple, and said to him, "If you are the Son of God, throw yourself down
from here, for it is written:

> *He will command his angels concerning you, to guard you,*

and:

> *With their hands they will support you,*
> *lest you dash your foot against a stone."*

Jesus said to him in reply, "It also says, *You shall not put the Lord, your
God, to the test.*" When the devil had finished every temptation, he
departed from him for a time.

First Reading (Deut 26:4-10)

Moses spoke to the people, saying: "The priest shall receive the basket
from you and shall set it in front of the altar of the LORD, your God. Then
you shall declare before the LORD, your God, 'My father was a wandering
Aramean who went down to Egypt with a small household and lived
there as an alien. But there he became a nation great, strong, and numerous. When the Egyptians maltreated and oppressed us, imposing hard
labor upon us, we cried to the LORD, the God of our fathers, and he heard
our cry and saw our affliction, our toil, and our oppression. He brought

us out of Egypt with his strong hand and outstretched arm, with terrifying power, with signs and wonders; and bringing us into this country, he gave us this land flowing with milk and honey. Therefore, I have now brought you the firstfruits of the products of the soil which you, O LORD, have given me.' And having set them before the LORD, your God, you shall bow down in his presence."

Responsorial Psalm (Ps 91:1-2, 10-11, 12-13, 14-15)

R̸. (cf. 15b) Be with me, Lord, when I am in trouble.

You who dwell in the shelter of the Most High,
    who abide in the shadow of the Almighty,
say to the LORD, "My refuge and fortress,
    my God in whom I trust."

R̸. Be with me, Lord, when I am in trouble.

No evil shall befall you,
    nor shall affliction come near your tent,
for to his angels he has given command about you,
    that they guard you in all your ways.

R̸. Be with me, Lord, when I am in trouble.

Upon their hands they shall bear you up,
    lest you dash your foot against a stone.
You shall tread upon the asp and the viper;
    you shall trample down the lion and the dragon.

R̸. Be with me, Lord, when I am in trouble.

Because he clings to me, I will deliver him;
    I will set him on high because he acknowledges my name.
He shall call upon me, and I will answer him;
    I will be with him in distress;
I will deliver him and glorify him.

R̸. Be with me, Lord, when I am in trouble.

See Appendix, p. 211, for Second Reading

Reflecting on Living the Gospel

The encounter of Jesus with "the devil" parallels our own encounters with "the devil." None of us—not even the God-Man—is exempt from temptation. By resisting the devil's temptations to act as "the Son of God," Jesus fully embraces his human identity. By resisting the devil's temptations to act against who God created us to be, we fully embrace our own human identity: graced beings created in the image of God.

Connecting the Responsorial Psalm to the Readings

As the psalm refrain indicates, Jesus is in "trouble." Hungry after forty days of fasting, he is accosted by Satan with every possible temptation. Yet he steadfastly "clings" to God (psalm). He chooses to "bow down" (first reading) only before God; he chooses to live not by bread, but by the word of God; he refuses to test God, but chooses to trust instead on a guarantee already given (psalm). Jesus' mission will lead to his death, but he knows God will "deliver him and glorify him" because this is what God has promised to do. Jesus remains true to who he is because he knows he can count on God remaining true to who God is. As we enter this new season of Lent, our forty-day testing period, we sing this psalm with Jesus and stand with him on God's promise.

Psalmist Preparation

As you enter this new Lenten season, this is a good time to examine how you may be tempted at times to misuse your power as psalmist. When are you tempted to focus the assembly's attention on yourself rather than on the psalm? When are you tempted to use your position to dominate the assembly rather than serve them? When you are so tempted, how does Christ keep you faithful to discipleship and service?

Prayer

Protector God, be with us as we enter this Lenten season of prayer and penance. Strengthen our resolve that we may, like Jesus, withstand temptation and serve only you. We ask this in his name. Amen.

***Gospel* (Luke 9:28b-36; L27C)**

Jesus took Peter, John, and James and went up the mountain to pray. While he was praying his face changed in appearance and his clothing became dazzling white. And behold, two men were conversing with him, Moses and Elijah, who appeared in glory and spoke of his exodus that he was going to accomplish in Jerusalem. Peter and his companions had been overcome by sleep, but becoming fully awake, they saw his glory and the two men standing with him. As they were about to part from him, Peter said to Jesus, "Master, it is good that we are here; let us make three tents, one for you, one for Moses, and one for Elijah." But he did not know what he was saying. While he was still speaking, a cloud came and cast a shadow over them, and they became frightened when they entered the cloud. Then from the cloud came a voice that said, "This is my chosen Son; listen to him." After the voice had spoken, Jesus was found alone. They fell silent and did not at that time tell anyone what they had seen.

***First Reading* (Gen 15:5-12, 17-18)**

The Lord God took Abram outside and said, "Look up at the sky and count the stars, if you can. Just so," he added, "shall your descendants be." Abram put his faith in the LORD, who credited it to him as an act of righteousness.

He then said to him, "I am the LORD who brought you from Ur of the Chaldeans to give you this land as a possession." "O Lord GOD," he asked, "how am I to know that I shall possess it?" He answered him, "Bring me a three-year-old heifer, a three-year-old she-goat, a three-year-old ram, a turtledove, and a young pigeon." Abram brought him all these, split them in two, and placed each half opposite the other; but the birds he did not cut up. Birds of prey swooped down on the carcasses, but Abram stayed with them. As the sun was about to set, a trance fell upon Abram, and a deep, terrifying darkness enveloped him.

When the sun had set and it was dark, there appeared a smoking fire pot and a flaming torch, which passed between those pieces. It was on that occasion that the LORD made a covenant with Abram, saying: "To your descendants I give this land, from the Wadi of Egypt to the Great River, the Euphrates."

Responsorial Psalm (Ps 27:1, 7-8, 8-9, 13-14)

R̠⁊. (1a) The Lord is my light and my salvation.

The LORD is my light and my salvation;
    whom should I fear?
The LORD is my life's refuge;
    of whom should I be afraid?

R̠⁊. The Lord is my light and my salvation.

Hear, O LORD, the sound of my call;
    have pity on me, and answer me.
Of you my heart speaks; you my glance seeks.

R̠⁊. The Lord is my light and my salvation.

Your presence, O LORD, I seek.
    Hide not your face from me;
do not in anger repel your servant.
    You are my helper: cast me not off.

R̠⁊. The Lord is my light and my salvation.

I believe that I shall see the bounty of the LORD
    in the land of the living.
Wait for the LORD with courage;
    be stouthearted, and wait for the LORD.

R̠⁊. The Lord is my light and my salvation.

See Appendix, p. 211, for Second Reading

Reflecting on Living the Gospel

Moses and Elijah speak of exodus, of going forth to Jerusalem; by contrast, Peter speaks of pitching tents, of staying on the mountain in the moment of glory. He chooses to stay with the beauty and wonder of the glory he sees, but by doing so he would deny his own share in this same glory. Are we to stay or to go? Both! Disciples must stay in Jesus' Presence and "listen to him," *and* go to their own Jerusalem to pass over from death to new Life.

Connecting the Responsorial Psalm to the Readings

Sung in a Lenten context, these verses from Psalm 27 remind us that the fearlessness that comes from knowing God is our salvation will not spare us from the reality of suffering and death. The transfigured Jesus glowed with the divine light (gospel) of God, our "light and [our] salvation" (psalm refrain). Jesus could face the "terrifying darkness" (first reading) of his passion and death because he counted on the covenant relationship God had established. In singing these psalm verses, we, like Jesus, make God the center and focus of our lives. Like Jesus we choose to undergo the "exodus" (gospel) required of us. And like him we, too, shall be transformed into glory by the light of God (second reading).

Psalmist Preparation

As part of your preparation to sing this responsorial psalm, read and pray with the whole of Psalm 27. Filled with images of danger and death, the psalm nonetheless maintains its confidence in God's ultimate promise of life. For you as a baptized Christian the danger is the struggle with evil, and the death is dying to self. How are you being called this Lent to this dying? How are you experiencing God's promise of resurrection?

Prayer

Lord, in the midst of sin and death you are our light and our salvation. As we walk our Lenten journey to the cross, grant us glimpses of the glory to which you are leading us so that we may walk with courage and persevere in hope. We ask this through Christ our Lord. Amen.

FEBRUARY 28, 2016

The readings given for Year A may be used in place of these.

Gospel (Luke 13:1-9; L30C)

Some people told Jesus about the Galileans whose blood Pilate had mingled with the blood of their sacrifices. Jesus said to them in reply, "Do you think that because these Galileans suffered in this way they were greater sinners than all other Galileans? By no means! But I tell you, if you do not repent, you will all perish as they did! Or those eighteen people who were killed when the tower at Siloam fell on them—do you think they were more guilty than everyone else who lived in Jerusalem? By no means! But I tell you, if you do not repent, you will all perish as they did!"

And he told them this parable: "There once was a person who had a fig tree planted in his orchard, and when he came in search of fruit on it but found none, he said to the gardener, 'For three years now I have come in search of fruit on this fig tree but have found none. So cut it down. Why should it exhaust the soil?' He said to him in reply, 'Sir, leave it for this year also, and I shall cultivate the ground around it and fertilize it; it may bear fruit in the future. If not you can cut it down.'"

First Reading (Exod 3:1-8a, 13-15)

Moses was tending the flock of his father-in-law Jethro, the priest of Midian. Leading the flock across the desert, he came to Horeb, the mountain of God. There an angel of the LORD appeared to Moses in fire flaming out of a bush. As he looked on, he was surprised to see that the bush, though on fire, was not consumed. So Moses decided, "I must go over to look at this remarkable sight, and see why the bush is not burned."

When the LORD saw him coming over to look at it more closely, God called out to him from the bush, "Moses! Moses!" He answered, "Here I am." God said, "Come no nearer! Remove the sandals from your feet, for the place where you stand is holy ground. I am the God of your fathers," he continued, "the God of Abraham, the God of Isaac, the God of Jacob." Moses hid his face, for he was afraid to look at God. But the LORD said, "I have witnessed the affliction of my people in Egypt and have heard their cry of complaint against their slave drivers, so I know well what they are suffering. Therefore I have come down to rescue them from the hands of the Egyptians and lead them out of that land into a good and spacious land, a land flowing with milk and honey."

Moses said to God, "But when I go to the Israelites and say to them, 'The God of your fathers has sent me to you,' if they ask me, 'What is his name?' what am I to tell them?" God replied, "I am who am." Then he added, "This is what you shall tell the Israelites: I AM sent me to you."

God spoke further to Moses, "Thus shall you say to the Israelites: The LORD, the God of your fathers, the God of Abraham, the God of Isaac, the God of Jacob, has sent me to you.

"This is my name forever;
    thus am I to be remembered through all generations."

Responsorial Psalm (Ps 103:1-2, 3-4, 6-7, 8, 11)

R̸. (8a) The Lord is kind and merciful.

Bless the LORD, O my soul;
    and all my being, bless his holy name.
Bless the LORD, O my soul,
    and forget not all his benefits.

R̸. The Lord is kind and merciful.

He pardons all your iniquities,
    he heals all your ills.
He redeems your life from destruction,
    he crowns you with kindness and compassion.

R̸. The Lord is kind and merciful.

The LORD secures justice
    and the rights of all the oppressed.
He has made known his ways to Moses,
    and his deeds to the children of Israel.

R̸. The Lord is kind and merciful.

Merciful and gracious is the LORD,
    slow to anger and abounding in kindness.
For as the heavens are high above the earth,
    so surpassing is his kindness toward those who fear him.

R̸. The Lord is kind and merciful.

See Appendix, p. 211, for Second Reading

Reflecting on Living the Gospel
Jesus attacks a misconception his hearers held: tragic death—and illness or other misfortunes—are not the result of sinning. Sinning is always our own choice, not a consequence of some impersonal outside force. Jesus issues a clear warning: sinfulness is not to be ignored—we must repent and bear the good fruit of right living. If not, we will perish. The work of Lent is to choose the eternal Life God continuously cultivates within us. God never gives up on us.

Connecting the Responsorial Psalm to the Readings
This Sunday's gospel and second reading require that we repent and do so immediately. The demand is unequivocal: if we do not repent we shall perish. Yet in the parable of the fig tree, Jesus seems to soften this demand when he reveals that God will always give us one more chance. The psalm tells us why: God is infinitely merciful, compassionate, kind, and forgiving. God is not vindictive, but "slow to anger" and quick to "pardon." The way to repentance, then, is to reach out and receive the gracious mercy God steadfastly offers us. Our task during Lent is to let our hearts be cultivated by One whose mercy and care will transform what is barren within us to new life. May our singing about this God whose mercy knows no bounds motivate our repentance and keep us faithful to the task at hand.

Psalmist Preparation
While the gospel demands you repent and the second reading warns you not to take salvation for granted, the responsorial psalm reminds you of God's mercy and compassion. The message, however, is not "do what you will and know you'll be forgiven" but "let us be faithful to this God who loves us so much." How does this message motivate your own repentance? How does it keep you faithful to the Lenten task of conversion of heart?

Prayer
Merciful God, you call us to repentance, pardoning all our sins and crowning us with kindness and compassion. Draw us to yourself that we may embrace your mercy and walk in newness of life. We ask this through Christ our Lord. Amen.

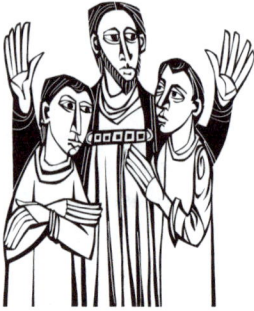

The readings for Year A may be used in place of these.

Gospel (Luke 15:1-3, 11-32; L33C)

Tax collectors and sinners were all drawing near to listen to Jesus, but the Pharisees and scribes began to complain, saying, "This man welcomes sinners and eats with them." So to them Jesus addressed this parable: "A man had two sons, and the younger son said to his father, 'Father give me the share of your estate that should come to me.' So the father divided the property between them. After a few days, the younger son collected all his belongings and set off to a distant country where he squandered his inheritance on a life of dissipation. When he had freely spent everything, a severe famine struck that country, and he found himself in dire need. So he hired himself out to one of the local citizens who sent him to his farm to tend the swine. And he longed to eat his fill of the pods on which the swine fed, but nobody gave him any. Coming to his senses he thought, 'How many of my father's hired workers have more than enough food to eat, but here am I, dying from hunger. I shall get up and go to my father and I shall say to him, "Father, I have sinned against heaven and against you. I no longer deserve to be called your son; treat me as you would treat one of your hired workers."' So he got up and went back to his father. While he was still a long way off, his father caught sight of him, and was filled with compassion. He ran to his son, embraced him and kissed him. His son said to him, 'Father, I have sinned against heaven and against you; I no longer deserve to be called your son.' But his father ordered his servants, 'Quickly bring the finest robe and put it on him; put a ring on his finger and sandals on his feet. Take the fattened calf and slaughter it. Then let us celebrate with a feast, because this son of mine was dead, and has come to life again; he was lost, and has been found.' Then the celebration began. Now the older son had been out in the field and, on his way back, as he neared the house, he heard the sound of music and dancing. He called one of the servants and asked what this might mean. The servant said to him, 'Your brother has returned and your father has slaughtered the fattened calf because he has him back safe and sound.' He became angry, and when he refused to enter the house, his father came out and pleaded with him. He said to his father in reply, 'Look, all these years I served you and not once did I disobey your orders; yet you never gave me even a young goat to feast on with my friends. But when your son returns who swallowed up your property with prostitutes, for him you slaughter the fattened calf.' He said to him, 'My son, you are here with me always; everything I have is yours. But now we must celebrate and rejoice, because your brother was dead and has come to life again; he was lost and has been found.'"

First Reading (Josh 5:9a, 10-12)

The LORD said to Joshua, "Today I have removed the reproach of Egypt from you."

While the Israelites were encamped at Gilgal on the plains of Jericho, they celebrated the Passover on the evening of the fourteenth of the month. On the day after the Passover, they ate of the produce of the land in the form of unleavened cakes and parched grain. On that same day after the Passover, on which they ate of the produce of the land, the manna ceased. No longer was there manna for the Israelites, who that year ate of the yield of the land of Canaan.

Responsorial Psalm (Ps 34:2-3, 4-5, 6-7)

R℣. (9a) Taste and see the goodness of the Lord.

I will bless the LORD at all times;
    his praise shall be ever in my mouth.
Let my soul glory in the LORD;
    the lowly will hear me and be glad.

R℣. Taste and see the goodness of the Lord.

Glorify the LORD with me,
    let us together extol his name.
I sought the LORD, and he answered me
    and delivered me from all my fears.

R℣. Taste and see the goodness of the Lord.

Look to him that you may be radiant with joy,
    and your faces may not blush with shame.
When the poor one called out, the LORD heard,
    and from all his distress he saved him.

R℣. Taste and see the goodness of the Lord.

See Appendix, p. 212, for Second Reading

Reflecting on Living the Gospel

According to "the Pharisees and scribes," Jesus entertained all the wrong people! In the parable, the prodigal son entertained all the wrong desires! The elder son entertained anger and jealousy, pettiness and closed heartedness! On the other hand, the father tendered reconciliation leading to feasting. In our lives, God tenders mercy and forgiveness leading to new Life. What do we entertain in our hearts? What do we tender in our relationships? With whom do we feast?

Connecting the Responsorial Psalm to the Readings

In praying these verses from Psalm 34, we proclaim that we have tasted the goodness of the Lord. We know what it means to be the lowly who cry out to God for help and receive salvation. We join the enslaved Israelites who survived the terrible desert journey and feasted in the land of God's deliverance (first reading). We become the distant and dissipated prodigal son who crossed the terrain of regret and repentance and feasted at his father's table (gospel). We become a new creation in Christ (second reading), made ambassadors of the message: repent, come home, the feast is ready and—oh, so good—it is God!

Psalmist Preparation

The verses of this responsorial psalm arise from personal experience of the God who leads from famine to feast (first reading), from sin to reconciliation (gospel). What experience of God's goodness and mercy will shape your singing of this psalm? What radiance will shine on your face?

Prayer

Father of compassion and mercy, you long for our return whenever we stray from you. Help us to "come to our senses," hurry home, and sit down to your feast of forgiveness. We ask this through Christ our Lord. Amen.

The readings given for Year A may be used in place of these.

Gospel (John 8:1-11; L36C)

Jesus went to the Mount of Olives. But early in the morning he arrived again in the temple area, and all the people started coming to him, and he sat down and taught them. Then the scribes and the Pharisees brought a woman who had been caught in adultery and made her stand in the middle. They said to him, "Teacher, this woman was caught in the very act of committing adultery. Now in the law, Moses commanded us to stone such women. So what do you say?" They said this to test him, so that they could have some charge to bring against him. Jesus bent down and began to write on the ground with his finger. But when they continued asking him, he straightened up and said to them, "Let the one among you who is without sin be the first to throw a stone at her." Again he bent down and wrote on the ground. And in response, they went away one by one, beginning with the elders. So he was left alone with the woman before him. Then Jesus straightened up and said to her, "Woman, where are they? Has no one condemned you?" She replied, "No one, sir." Then Jesus said, "Neither do I condemn you. Go, and from now on do not sin any more."

First Reading (Isa 43:16-21)

Thus says the LORD,
   who opens a way in the sea
   and a path in the mighty waters,
who leads out chariots and horsemen,
   a powerful army,
till they lie prostrate together, never to rise,
   snuffed out and quenched like a wick.
Remember not the events of the past,
   the things of long ago consider not;
see, I am doing something new!
   Now it springs forth, do you not perceive it?
In the desert I make a way,
   in the wasteland, rivers.
Wild beasts honor me,
   jackals and ostriches,

for I put water in the desert
and rivers in the wasteland
for my chosen people to drink,
the people whom I formed for myself,
that they might announce my praise.

Responsorial Psalm (Ps 126:1-2, 2-3, 4-5, 6)

R̊. (3) The Lord has done great things for us; we are filled with joy.

When the LORD brought back the captives of Zion,
we were like men dreaming.
Then our mouth was filled with laughter,
and our tongue with rejoicing.

R̊. The Lord has done great things for us; we are filled with joy.

Then they said among the nations,
"The LORD has done great things for them."
The LORD has done great things for us;
we are glad indeed.

R̊. The Lord has done great things for us; we are filled with joy.

Restore our fortunes, O LORD,
like the torrents in the southern desert.
Those that sow in tears
shall reap rejoicing.

R̊. The Lord has done great things for us; we are filled with joy.

Although they go forth weeping,
carrying the seed to be sown,
they shall come back rejoicing,
carrying their sheaves.

R̊. The Lord has done great things for us; we are filled with joy.

See Appendix, p. 212, for Second Reading

Reflecting on Living the Gospel

The "scribes and the Pharisees" use the proscription of the law in an attempt to entrap Jesus. He responds by confronting them with the reality of their own hard-heartedness and sinfulness. They slink away "one by one," leaving the adulterous woman alone to face Jesus. He extends mercy and compassion as well as judgment and a command to change her life. Do we dare to stand alone before Jesus, bare our own sinfulness, and hear him say to us, "Go, and from now on do not sin any more"?

Connecting the Responsorial Psalm to the Readings

The first reading from Isaiah recounts God's mighty acts in restoring Israel as a nation after the Babylonian captivity. As Isaiah asserts, this restoration will make the exodus look as if it were nothing ("Remember not the events of the past . . . I am doing something new!"). The gospel reading recounts God's acting again to do something new in Jesus. Salvation becomes personalized in the adulterous woman whom Jesus does not condemn but grants new life, both physically and spiritually.

God constantly revolutionizes our expectations by saving us in newer, deeper ways. Psalm 126 is our "pinch me" response: we are not dreaming; this salvation is really happening. The readings remind us, however, that the challenge is not just to see but to believe. We must let this new righteousness take possession of us (second reading). We must change our ways and let go of our judgments (gospel). Only then can we "forget . . . what lies behind" and look toward the future (second reading). Only then can we realize the past about which we sing is just the beginning.

Psalmist Preparation

As you sing this psalm you do not just retell past events; you establish hope for the future. The great things God has already done are as nothing compared to what God is yet to do for us in Christ. In what way this week might you let Christ take possession of you (second reading) so that you can sing of this hope with conviction?

Prayer

God of new beginnings, you call us to forget what lies behind so that we may embrace our future in you. Help us this Lent to relinquish whatever in our lives prevents us from becoming the persons you call us to be. We ask this through Christ our Lord. Amen.

Gospel at the procession with palms
(Luke 19:28-40; L37C)

Gospel at Mass **(Luke 22:14–23:56 [or Luke 23:1-49]; L38ABC)**

First Reading **(Isa 50:4-7)**

> The Lord God has given me
> a well-trained tongue,
> that I might know how to speak to the weary
> a word that will rouse them.
> Morning after morning
> he opens my ear that I may hear;
> and I have not rebelled,
> have not turned back.
> I gave my back to those who beat me,
> my cheeks to those who plucked my beard;
> my face I did not shield
> from buffets and spitting.
>
> The Lord God is my help,
> therefore I am not disgraced;
> I have set my face like flint,
> knowing that I shall not be put to shame.

Responsorial Psalm **(Ps 22:8-9, 17-18, 19-20, 23-24)**

℟. (2a) My God, my God, why have you abandoned me?

All who see me scoff at me;
  they mock me with parted lips, they wag their heads:
"He relied on the Lord; let him deliver him,
  let him rescue him, if he loves him."

℟. My God, my God, why have you abandoned me?

Indeed, many dogs surround me,
  a pack of evildoers closes in upon me;
they have pierced my hands and my feet;
  I can count all my bones.

℟. My God, my God, why have you abandoned me?

They divide my garments among them,
  and for my vesture they cast lots.

But you, O LORD, be not far from me;
O my help, hasten to aid me.

R̸. My God, my God, why have you abandoned me?

I will proclaim your name to my brethren;
in the midst of the assembly I will praise you:
"You who fear the LORD, praise him;
all you descendants of Jacob, give glory to him;
revere him, all you descendants of Israel!"

R̸. My God, my God, why have you abandoned me?

See Appendix, p. 212, for Second Reading

Reflecting on Living the Gospel

Neither the Jewish leadership, the Roman leadership, nor the apostles
understand. Throughout Luke's passion account, Jesus is trying to turn
his accusers and hearers away from their understanding of kingdom to
embracing "the kingdom of God." Even on the cross, he continues to
show how different his kingdom is, for he forgives the very ones who
cause him suffering and death. The gift of his death? He confers on us
his kingdom and invites us to be with him in Paradise.

Connecting the Responsorial Psalm to the Readings

The whole of Psalm 22 is a masterpiece of poetry and theology. The
psalmist struggles with an increasing sense of being abandoned (from
"My God, my God, why have you abandoned me" to "All who see me
scoff at me" to violent imagery of destruction and death) while also experiencing deepening intimacy with God (the one who is far away and
does not answer is also the one who has been present "from [my mother's] womb"; v. 10). The psalmist begs to be saved from suffering and violence, then offers God lengthy praise. Most lament psalms end with one
or two short verses of praise, but here the praise continues for nearly
one-third of the text. Furthermore, the psalmist invites an ever-widening
circle to join in the praise: first the psalmist's immediate family, then all
of Israel, then all nations, then generations yet unborn, and, finally, even
the dead.

Psalm 22 helps us understand the passion, both Christ's and ours. God
is not distant from the suffering, but very near. And the depth of the suffering becomes the wellspring of the most profound praise. May our

singing of these verses from Psalm 22 give us the courage we need to enter Holy Week aware of both the pain and the praise, the loss and the glory, to which it will lead.

Psalmist Preparation

To sing this psalm well, you must take some time to pray the full text of Psalm 22. You sing not only about Christ's suffering but about his transformation into risen Life through his suffering and death. You sing about your own transformation as well, for through baptism you have been incorporated into Jesus' death and resurrection. How willing are you to undergo this transformation? How willing are you to invite the assembly to do so?

Prayer

Redeeming God, you sent your Son to teach us to overcome death by willingly accepting it for the sake of others. Be with us as we enter this holiest week of the year. Give us the courage we need to walk with Jesus to the cross and to the glory beyond. We ask this through Christ our Lord. Amen.

MARCH 24, 2016

Gospel (John 13:1-15; L39ABC)

Before the feast of Passover, Jesus knew that his hour had come to pass from this world to the Father. He loved his own in the world and he loved them to the end. The devil had already induced Judas, son of Simon the Iscariot, to hand him over. So, during supper, fully aware that the Father had put everything into his power and that he had come from God and was returning to God, he rose from supper and took off his outer garments. He took a towel and tied it around his waist. Then he poured water into a basin and began to wash the disciples' feet and dry them with the towel around his waist. He came to Simon Peter, who said to him, "Master, are you going to wash my feet?" Jesus answered and said to him, "What I am doing, you do not understand now, but you will understand later." Peter said to him, "You will never wash my feet." Jesus answered him, "Unless I wash you, you will have no inheritance with me." Simon Peter said to him, "Master, then not only my feet, but my hands and head as well." Jesus said to him, "Whoever has bathed has no need except to have his feet washed, for he is clean all over; so you are clean, but not all." For he knew who would betray him; for this reason, he said, "Not all of you are clean."

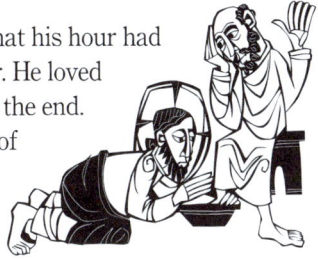

So when he had washed their feet and put his garments back on and reclined at table again, he said to them, "Do you realize what I have done for you? You call me 'teacher' and 'master,' and rightly so, for indeed I am. If I, therefore, the master and teacher, have washed your feet, you ought to wash one another's feet. I have given you a model to follow, so that as I have done for you, you should also do."

First Reading (Exod 12:1-8, 11-14)

The LORD said to Moses and Aaron in the land of Egypt, "This month shall stand at the head of your calendar; you shall reckon it the first month of the year. Tell the whole community of Israel: On the tenth of this month every one of your families must procure for itself a lamb, one apiece for each household. If a family is too small for a whole lamb, it shall join the nearest household in procuring one and shall share in the lamb in proportion to the number of persons who partake of it. The lamb must be a year-old male and without blemish. You may take it from either the sheep or the goats. You shall keep it until the fourteenth day of this month, and then, with the whole assembly of Israel present, it shall be slaughtered during the evening twilight. They shall take some of its blood and apply it to the two doorposts and the lintel of every house in which they partake of the lamb. That same night they shall eat its roasted flesh with unleavened bread and bitter herbs.

"This is how you are to eat it: with your loins girt, sandals on your feet and your staff in hand, you shall eat like those who are in flight. It is the Passover of the LORD. For on this same night I will go through Egypt, striking down every firstborn of the land, both man and beast, and executing judgment on all the gods of Egypt—I, the LORD! But the blood will mark the houses where you are. Seeing the blood, I will pass over you; thus, when I strike the land of Egypt, no destructive blow will come upon you.

"This day shall be a memorial feast for you, which all your generations shall celebrate with pilgrimage to the LORD, as a perpetual institution."

Responsorial Psalm (Ps 116:12-13, 15-16bc, 17-18)

R̶7. (cf. 1 Cor 10:16) Our blessing-cup is a communion with the Blood of Christ.

How shall I make a return to the LORD
    for all the good he has done for me?
The cup of salvation I will take up,
    and I will call upon the name of the LORD.

R̶7. Our blessing-cup is a communion with the Blood of Christ.

Precious in the eyes of the LORD
    is the death of his faithful ones.
I am your servant, the son of your handmaid;
    you have loosed my bonds.

R̶7. Our blessing-cup is a communion with the Blood of Christ.

To you will I offer sacrifice of thanksgiving,
    and I will call upon the name of the LORD.
My vows to the LORD I will pay
    in the presence of all his people.

R̶7. Our blessing-cup is a communion with the Blood of Christ.

See Appendix, p. 213, for Second Reading

Reflecting on Living the Gospel

Jesus sums up in the simple action of washing feet what his whole life and ministry have been about. The profound message Jesus proclaimed by his faith-in-action is the extent of his love—"he loved them to the end." Jesus' self-sacrificing love is not simply a word but is deeds for the sake of others. Loving is serving; loving is spilling out our very body and blood for others. Pouring forth one's body and blood is indeed an act of Eucharist—it is giving oneself for another's life.

Connecting the Responsorial Psalm to the Readings

The "blessing-cup" about which we sing in the psalm refrain was the third cup drunk as part of the Jewish Passover meal. Those who shared this cup were united with each other and God. On Holy Thursday—and at every celebration of the Eucharist—the "blessing-cup" we drink is the Blood of Christ, source of our salvation. By drinking this cup we take the Blood of Christ into ourselves and become one with him in his death and resurrection. Drinking this cup does not save us *from* death but *through* death, a death freely chosen in self-giving service to one another (gospel). By drinking it we not only "proclaim the death of the Lord" (second reading); we unite ourselves with him, and with one another, in his death, and find salvation.

Psalmist Preparation

What are the "vows to the LORD" you pay in drinking the blessing-cup of Christ's Blood? Certainly, you thank God for saving your life through Christ. But you also promise to become one with Christ in losing your life for the sake of others. You promise to become the servant who washes feet. Are you willing to do this? Whose feet need washing?

Prayer

Redeeming God, you call us to communion in the Blood of Christ. May our drinking of his cup lead us always to serve one another in generous and joyful love. We ask this in his name. Amen.

Gospel (John 18:1–19:42; L40ABC)

First Reading (Isa 52:13–53:12)

See, my servant shall prosper,
    he shall be raised high and greatly exalted.
Even as many were amazed at him—
    so marred was his look beyond human
        semblance
and his appearance beyond that of the sons of man—
so shall he startle many nations, because of him
    kings shall stand speechless;
for those who have not been told shall see,
    those who have not heard shall ponder it.

Who would believe what we have heard?
    To whom has the arm of the LORD been revealed?
He grew up like a sapling before him,
    like a shoot from the parched earth;
there was in him no stately bearing to make us look at him,
    nor appearance that would attract us to him.
He was spurned and avoided by people,
    a man of suffering, accustomed to infirmity,
one of those from whom people hide their faces,
    spurned, and we held him in no esteem.

Yet it was our infirmities that he bore,
    our sufferings that he endured,
while we thought of him as stricken,
    as one smitten by God and afflicted.
But he was pierced for our offenses,
    crushed for our sins;
upon him was the chastisement that makes us whole,
    by his stripes we were healed.
We had all gone astray like sheep,
    each following his own way;
but the LORD laid upon him
    the guilt of us all.

Though he was harshly treated, he submitted
  and opened not his mouth;
like a lamb led to the slaughter
  or a sheep before the shearers,
    he was silent and opened not his mouth.
Oppressed and condemned, he was taken away,
  and who would have thought any more of his destiny?
When he was cut off from the land of the living,
  and smitten for the sin of his people,
a grave was assigned him among the wicked
  and a burial place with evildoers,
though he had done no wrong
  nor spoken any falsehood.
But the LORD was pleased
  to crush him in infirmity.

If he gives his life as an offering for sin,
  he shall see his descendants in a long life,
  and the will of the LORD shall be accomplished through him.

Because of his affliction
  he shall see the light in fullness of days;
through his suffering, my servant shall justify many,
  and their guilt he shall bear.
Therefore I will give him his portion among the great,
  and he shall divide the spoils with the mighty,
because he surrendered himself to death
  and was counted among the wicked;
and he shall take away the sins of many,
  and win pardon for their offenses.

Responsorial Psalm (Ps 31:2, 6, 12-13, 15-16, 17, 25)

℞. (Luke 23:46) Father, into your hands I commend my spirit.

In you, O LORD, I take refuge;
  let me never be put to shame.
In your justice rescue me.
Into your hands I commend my spirit;
  you will redeem me, O LORD, O faithful God.

℞. Father, into your hands I commend my spirit.

For all my foes I am an object of reproach,
>   a laughingstock to my neighbors, and a dread to my friends;
>   they who see me abroad flee from me.
I am forgotten like the unremembered dead;
>   I am like a dish that is broken.

R⁊. Father, into your hands I commend my spirit.

But my trust is in you, O LORD;
>   I say, "You are my God.
In your hands is my destiny; rescue me
>   from the clutches of my enemies and my persecutors."

R⁊. Father, into your hands I commend my spirit.

Let your face shine upon your servant;
>   save me in your kindness.
Take courage and be stouthearted,
>   all you who hope in the LORD.

R⁊. Father, into your hands I commend my spirit.

See Appendix, p. 213, for Second Reading

Reflecting on Living the Gospel

Good Friday is more than a step to resurrection; it is a day on which we celebrate Jesus' obedience, his kingship, the everlasting establishment of his reign, his side being opened and himself being poured out so that we can be washed in his very blood and water. The real scandal of the cross isn't suffering and death; the real scandal of the cross is that death is vanquished by Jesus' self-giving, visible love. Death has no power over God.

Connecting the Responsorial Psalm to the Readings

Psalm 31 is a poignant lament in which someone persecuted by enemies calls trustfully to God for help and then sings thanksgiving to God for salvation. Onlookers consider this person a fool ("laughingstock"), fearful to look at ("a dread"), someone best "forgotten." But to God this person is a faithful servant for whom God will always be the faithful redeemer. The Lectionary places words from Psalm 31 on the lips of Jesus, and frames his prayer with the refrain, "Father, into your hands I commend my spirit." Jesus' "spirit" is both his life-breath and the orientation of his heart. Amidst the unspeakable sufferings of his passion and death he continues to surrender himself, as he did all his life, to the Father in whose presence and care he trusts. The final verse stands as Jesus' words to us, and our words to all who remain faithful to God no matter what the personal cost: "Take courage . . . hope in the LORD."

Psalmist Preparation

You sing these words from Psalm 31 as one united with Jesus in his gift of self to the Father. In your singing you invite assembly members also to join themselves with Jesus. You encourage them in the final verse to remain "stouthearted" in their hope in the God of life and salvation. What keeps you stouthearted? How at this moment in your life do you need to give yourself over in obedience and trust to God? What gives you the courage to do so?

Prayer

God of salvation, in the life, death, and resurrection of your Son Jesus, you give over your Spirit to us. Open our hearts that, united with Jesus, we may return your gift by offering our spirit to you in obedience, trust, and love. We ask this through him, our Brother and Savior. Amen.

Additional readings can be found in the Lectionary for Mass.

Gospel (Luke 24:1-12; L41ABC)

At daybreak on the first day of the week the women who had come from Galilee with Jesus took the spices they had prepared and went to the tomb. They found the stone rolled away from the tomb; but when they entered, they did not find the body of the Lord Jesus. While they were puzzling over this, behold, two men in dazzling garments appeared to them. They were terrified and bowed their faces to the ground. They said to them, "Why do you seek the living one among the dead? He is not here, but he has been raised. Remember what he said to you while he was still in Galilee, that the Son of Man must be handed over to sinners and be crucified, and rise on the third day." And they remembered his words. Then they returned from the tomb and announced all these things to the eleven and to all the others. The women were Mary Magdalene, Joanna, and Mary the mother of James; the others who accompanied them also told this to the apostles, but their story seemed like nonsense and they did not believe them. But Peter got up and ran to the tomb, bent down, and saw the burial cloths alone; then he went home amazed at what had happened.

Epistle (Rom 6:3-11)

Brothers and sisters: Are you unaware that we who were baptized into Christ Jesus were baptized into his death? We were indeed buried with him through baptism into death, so that, just as Christ was raised from the dead by the glory of the Father, we too might live in newness of life.

For if we have grown into union with him through a death like his, we shall also be united with him in the resurrection. We know that our old self was crucified with him, so that our sinful body might be done away with, that we might no longer be in slavery to sin. For a dead person has been absolved from sin. If, then, we have died with Christ, we believe that we shall also live with him. We know that Christ, raised from the dead, dies no more; death no longer has power over him. As to his death, he died to sin once and for all; as to his life, he lives for God. Consequently, you too must think of yourselves as being dead to sin and living for God in Christ Jesus.

Responsorial Psalm (Ps 118:1-2, 16-17, 22-23)

R̸. Alleluia, alleluia, alleluia.

Give thanks to the LORD, for he is good,
    for his mercy endures forever.
Let the house of Israel say,
    "His mercy endures forever."

R̸. Alleluia, alleluia, alleluia.

"The right hand of the LORD has struck with power;
    the right hand of the LORD is exalted.
I shall not die, but live,
    and declare the works of the LORD."

R̸. Alleluia, alleluia, alleluia.

The stone which the builders rejected
    has become the cornerstone.
By the LORD has this been done;
    it is wonderful in our eyes.

R̸. Alleluia, alleluia, alleluia.

Reflecting on Living the Gospel
This is the night when Jesus passes from death to risen Life. This is the
night when our own being and doing collapse into a living faith that is
full, robust, eager to announce the Good News that death is overcome,
that our belief is not in vain, that Jesus lives on in us who are baptized.
This is the night—just this one night—when we can ignore the sting of
death because life is so abundant.

Connecting the Responsorial Psalm to the Readings
Psalm 118 was a hymn sung as the Israelites processed into the temple to
give thanks to God for saving them from destruction by an enemy. The
procession entailed a march through the streets during which a soloist
sang verses about facing death and a choir responded with verses about
God's intervention to save. Verses 14, 15-16 are drawn from Exodus 15,
indicating the Israelites saw every victory over an enemy as an extension
of the exodus event when God led them from slavery to freedom.

Psalm 118 is also our song of deliverance. Our saving event comes in
Christ with whom we have died and risen, and with whom we share
glory (epistle). Our call is to believe what has happened to Christ (gospel)
and become aware of what has happened to us (epistle). As we sing

Psalm 118, Christ is the soloist leading the song and we are the ones answering "Alleluia!"

Psalmist Preparation

Are you unaware that you have died and risen with Christ (see epistle)? You proclaim to the assembly the wonderful work done by God in Christ and also done in them. How might you communicate the joy you feel this day both for yourself and for them?

Prayer

Saving God, you raise us out of the darkness of sin and death to new life in your Son. May we always declare your saving works and live fully aware of what you have achieved in us. We ask this in his name. Amen.

Gospel **(John 20:1-9; L42ABC)**

On the first day of the week, Mary of Magdala came to the tomb early in the morning, while it was still dark, and saw the stone removed from the tomb. So she ran and went to Simon Peter and to the other disciple whom Jesus loved, and told them, "They have taken the Lord from the tomb, and we don't know where they put him." So Peter and the other disciple went out and came to the tomb. They both ran, but the other disciple ran faster than Peter and arrived at the tomb first; he bent down and saw the burial cloths there, but did not go in. When Simon Peter arrived after him, he went into the tomb and saw the burial cloths there, and the cloth that had covered his head, not with the burial cloths but rolled up in a separate place. Then the other disciple also went in, the one who had arrived at the tomb first, and he saw and believed. For they did not yet understand the Scripture that he had to rise from the dead.

or **Gospel (Luke 24:1-12; L41C)**

or **at an afternoon or evening Mass**
Gospel (Luke 24:13-35; L46)

First Reading **(Acts 10:34a, 37-43)**

Peter proceeded to speak and said: "You know what has happened all over Judea, beginning in Galilee after the baptism that John preached, how God anointed Jesus of Nazareth with the Holy Spirit and power. He went about doing good and healing all those oppressed by the devil, for God was with him. We are witnesses of all that he did both in the country of the Jews and in Jerusalem. They put him to death by hanging him on a tree. This man God raised on the third day and granted that he be visible, not to all the people, but to us, the witnesses chosen by God in advance, who ate and drank with him after he rose from the dead. He commissioned us to preach to the people and testify that he is the one appointed by God as judge of the living and the dead. To him all the prophets bear witness, that everyone who believes in him will receive forgiveness of sins through his name."

Responsorial Psalm **(Ps 118:1-2, 16-17, 22-23)**

℟. (24) This is the day the Lord has made; let us rejoice and be glad.
or: ℟. Alleluia.

Give thanks to the LORD, for he is good,
for his mercy endures forever.
Let the house of Israel say,
"His mercy endures forever."

℟. This is the day the Lord has made; let us rejoice and be glad.
or: ℟. Alleluia.

"The right hand of the LORD has struck with power;
the right hand of the LORD is exalted.
I shall not die, but live,
and declare the works of the LORD."

℟. This is the day the Lord has made; let us rejoice and be glad.
or: ℟. Alleluia.

The stone which the builders rejected
has become the cornerstone.
By the LORD has this been done;
it is wonderful in our eyes.

℟. This is the day the Lord has made; let us rejoice and be glad.
or: ℟. Alleluia.

See Appendix, p. 213, for Second Reading

Reflecting on Living the Gospel
It was "early in the morning, / while it was still dark" that Mary Magdalene went to the tomb. How did she see? How did she know? She ran to Peter and John and they ran to the tomb. They, too, saw. More than saw. Their seeing could penetrate the darkness of not understanding. Their seeing was a response of the heart that led to their believing. The mystery of the resurrection is able to be seen because God gives us eyes of faith.

Connecting the Responsorial Psalm to the Readings
Psalm 118 was a hymn sung as the Israelites processed into the temple to give thanks to God for saving them from destruction by an enemy. The procession entailed a march through the streets during which a soloist

sang verses about facing death and a choir responded with verses about God's intervention to save. Verses 14, 15-16 are drawn from Exodus 15, indicating the Israelites saw every victory over an enemy as an extension of the exodus event when God led them from slavery to freedom.

Psalm 118 is also our song of deliverance. Our saving event comes in Christ with whom we have died and risen, and with whom we share glory (second reading from Colossians). Our mission is to proclaim this work of God to all peoples (first reading). In singing Psalm 118 we do just that, calling all to rejoice in God's wonderful deeds.

Psalmist Preparation

In Psalm 118, the source of the responsorial psalm for Easter Sunday, a choir led the Israelites processing into the temple in their praise for God's mighty acts of salvation. This is your role, not only on Easter but every Sunday. In order to sing of God's saving deeds, however, you must know what they are. How have you experienced death and resurrection this Lent? How has your family experienced it? your parish? the world?

Prayer

All-powerful God, you raised your Son Jesus from the darkness of the tomb to the brightness of new life. Keep us united with him so that we, too, may be raised from death to new life. We ask this through him, our Brother and Savior. Amen.

Gospel (John 20:19-31; L45C)

On the evening of that first day of the week, when the doors were locked, where the disciples were, for fear of the Jews, Jesus came and stood in their midst and said to them, "Peace be with you." When he had said this, he showed them his hands and his side. The disciples rejoiced when they saw the Lord. Jesus said to them again, "Peace be with you. As the Father has sent me, so I send you." And when he had said this, he breathed on them and said to them, "Receive the Holy Spirit. Whose sins you forgive are forgiven them, and whose sins you retain are retained."

Thomas, called Didymus, one of the Twelve, was not with them when Jesus came. So the other disciples said to him, "We have seen the Lord." But he said to them, "Unless I see the mark of the nails in his hands and put my finger into the nailmarks and put my hand into his side, I will not believe."

Now a week later his disciples were again inside and Thomas was with them. Jesus came, although the doors were locked, and stood in their midst and said, "Peace be with you." Then he said to Thomas, "Put your finger here and see my hands, and bring your hand and put it into my side, and do not be unbelieving, but believe." Thomas answered and said to him, "My Lord and my God!" Jesus said to him, "Have you come to believe because you have seen me? Blessed are those who have not seen and have believed."

Now Jesus did many other signs in the presence of his disciples that are not written in this book. But these are written that you may come to believe that Jesus is the Christ, the Son of God, and that through this belief you may have life in his name.

First Reading (Acts 5:12-16)

Many signs and wonders were done among the people at the hands of the apostles. They were all together in Solomon's portico. None of the others dared to join them, but the people esteemed them. Yet more than ever, believers in the Lord, great numbers of men and women, were added to them. Thus they even carried the sick out into the streets and laid them on cots and mats so that when Peter came by, at least his shadow might fall on one or another of them. A large number of people from the towns in the vicinity of Jerusalem also gathered, bringing the sick and those disturbed by unclean spirits, and they were all cured.

Responsorial Psalm (Ps 118:2-4, 13-15, 22-24)

℟. (1) Give thanks to the Lord for he is good, his love is everlasting.
or: ℟. Alleluia.

Let the house of Israel say,
  "His mercy endures forever."
Let the house of Aaron say,
  "His mercy endures forever."
Let those who fear the LORD say,
  "His mercy endures forever."

℟. Give thanks to the Lord for he is good, his love is everlasting.
or: ℟. Alleluia.

I was hard pressed and was falling,
  but the LORD helped me.
My strength and my courage is the LORD,
  and he has been my savior.
The joyful shout of victory
  in the tents of the just.

℟. Give thanks to the Lord for he is good, his love is everlasting.
or: ℟. Alleluia.

The stone which the builders rejected
  has become the cornerstone.
By the LORD has this been done;
  it is wonderful in our eyes.
This is the day the LORD has made;
  let us be glad and rejoice in it.

℟. Give thanks to the Lord for he is good, his love is everlasting.
or: ℟. Alleluia.

See Appendix, p. 213, for Second Reading

Reflecting on Living the Gospel

When the risen Lord appears to the disciples locked away behind closed doors, fear is allayed by peace, sin is allayed by forgiveness, doubt is allayed by Presence, unbelieving is allayed by seeing-believing. We know *to whom and what* our belief is directed: to Jesus and the gift of risen

Life. We know *how* we receive risen Life: through Jesus' gift of the breath of the Holy Spirit dwelling within us. Risen Life is God's divine Life transforming who and how we are.

Connecting the Responsorial Psalm to the Readings

In these verses from Psalm 118, we invite an ever-widening circle to join in praising God for mercy and deliverance. We do so as the community of believers commissioned to "[w]rite down . . . what [we] have seen, / and what is happening, and what will happen afterwards" (second reading). What has happened and will continue to happen is God's victory over death (second reading), disease (first reading), and sin (gospel). God takes what is flawed, useless, and inconsequential—the rejected stone (psalm), our failing lives (psalm), our diseased bodies (first reading), our doubting hearts (gospel)—and makes them the cornerstone of faith and forgiveness. This is resurrection, done "by the Lord" and "wonderful in our eyes." And it happens every day in "signs and wonders" (first reading) both great and small. For this we "[g]ive thanks to the Lord" (psalm refrain).

Psalmist Preparation

In singing Psalm 118 you call the church to recognize and give thanks for the enduring mercy of God. You can only give a "joyful shout" because you have had personal experience of God's saving intervention, because you have been "hard pressed" and "falling" and known God's help. What story will you be telling when you sing?

Prayer

Almighty God, you raised Jesus to new life to show us your power over sin, suffering, and death. Take what is weak and broken in our lives and make these the source of new life and the foundation of our faith in you. We ask this through Christ our Lord. Amen.

Gospel (John 21:1-19 [or 21:1-14]; L48C)

At that time, Jesus revealed himself again to his disciples at the Sea of Tiberias. He revealed himself in this way. Together were Simon Peter, Thomas called Didymus, Nathanael from Cana in Galilee, Zebedee's sons, and two others of his disciples. Simon Peter said to them, "I am going fishing." They said to him, "We also will come with you." So they went out and got into the boat, but that night they caught nothing. When it was already dawn, Jesus was standing on the shore; but the disciples did not realize that it was Jesus. Jesus said to them, "Children, have you caught anything to eat?" They answered him, "No." So he said to them, "Cast the net over the right side of the boat and you will find something." So they cast it, and were not able to pull it in because of the number of fish. So the disciple whom Jesus loved said to Peter, "It is the Lord." When Simon Peter heard that it was the Lord, he tucked in his garment, for he was lightly clad, and jumped into the sea. The other disciples came in the boat, for they were not far from shore, only about a hundred yards, dragging the net with the fish. When they climbed out on shore, they saw a charcoal fire with fish on it and bread. Jesus said to them, "Bring some of the fish you just caught." So Simon Peter went over and dragged the net ashore full of one hundred fifty-three large fish. Even though there were so many, the net was not torn. Jesus said to them, "Come, have breakfast." And none of the disciples dared to ask him, "Who are you?" because they realized it was the Lord. Jesus came over and took the bread and gave it to them, and in like manner the fish. This was now the third time Jesus was revealed to his disciples after being raised from the dead.

When they had finished breakfast, Jesus said to Simon Peter, "Simon, son of John, do you love me more than these?" Simon Peter answered him, "Yes, Lord, you know that I love you." Jesus said to him, "Feed my lambs." He then said to Simon Peter a second time, "Simon, son of John, do you love me?" Simon Peter answered him, "Yes, Lord, you know that I love you." Jesus said to him, "Tend my sheep." Jesus said to him the third time, "Simon, son of John, do you love me?" Peter was distressed that Jesus had said to him a third time, "Do you love me?" and he said to him, "Lord, you know everything; you know that I love you." Jesus said to

him, "Feed my sheep. Amen, amen, I say to you, when you were younger, you used to dress yourself and go where you wanted; but when you grow old, you will stretch out your hands, and someone else will dress you and lead you where you do not want to go." He said this signifying by what kind of death he would glorify God. And when he had said this, he said to him, "Follow me."

First Reading (Acts 5:27-32, 40b-41)

When the captain and the court officers had brought the apostles in and made them stand before the Sanhedrin, the high priest questioned them, "We gave you strict orders, did we not, to stop teaching in that name? Yet you have filled Jerusalem with your teaching and want to bring this man's blood upon us." But Peter and the apostles said in reply, "We must obey God rather than men. The God of our ancestors raised Jesus, though you had him killed by hanging him on a tree. God exalted him at his right hand as leader and savior to grant Israel repentance and forgiveness of sins. We are witnesses of these things, as is the Holy Spirit whom God has given to those who obey him."

The Sanhedrin ordered the apostles to stop speaking in the name of Jesus, and dismissed them. So they left the presence of the Sanhedrin, rejoicing that they had been found worthy to suffer dishonor for the sake of the name.

Responsorial Psalm (Ps 30:2, 4, 5-6, 11-12, 13)

R℣. (2a) I will praise you, Lord, for you have rescued me. *or:* R℣. Alleluia.

I will extol you, O LORD, for you drew me clear
    and did not let my enemies rejoice over me.
O LORD, you brought me up from the netherworld;
    you preserved me from among those going down into the pit.

R℣. I will praise you, Lord, for you have rescued me. *or:* R℣. Alleluia.

Sing praise to the LORD, you his faithful ones,
    and give thanks to his holy name.
For his anger lasts but a moment;
    a lifetime, his good will.
At nightfall, weeping enters in,
    but with the dawn, rejoicing.

R℣. I will praise you, Lord, for you have rescued me. *or:* R℣. Alleluia.

Hear, O Lᴏʀᴅ, and have pity on me;
  O Lᴏʀᴅ, be my helper.
You changed my mourning into dancing;
  O Lᴏʀᴅ, my God, forever will I give you thanks.

℟. I will praise you, Lord, for you have rescued me. *or:* ℟. Alleluia.

See Appendix, p. 214, for Second Reading

Reflecting on Living the Gospel

The risen Christ transforms the way we are, enabling us to obey his on-going invitation, "Follow me." We are fortified by Jesus' risen Presence, by his invitation to follow, by his own love for us that transforms our love into faithfulness and fruitfulness. Risen Life fortifies us for the transformation needed on our discipleship journey of seeing-believing. Risen Life is given to us by Christ, but we must also seek it. Risen Life is a gift, but we must also grasp it.

Connecting the Responsorial Psalm to the Readings

Although probably written before the Babylonian exile, Psalm 30 was used at Chanukah, the annual festival commemorating the reconsecration of the temple after it had been desecrated by the Seleucid army. The psalm is a song of thanksgiving to God for restoration after destruction.

What is the restoration we celebrate this Sunday? Most obviously Jesus' resurrection from death. But also Peter's restoration to loving relationship with Jesus after his denial of him before the passion (gospel). Once fearful ot speaking up in Jesus' name, Peter now rejoices in the very suffering that doing so will bring him (first reading). With joy he joins the crowds in heaven who cry out in praise of the "Lamb that was slain" (second reading). In singing Psalm 30 we make Peter's restoration our restoration. We celebrate that we, too, have been "brought . . . up from the netherworld" of sin, infidelity, and fear of death to a new life of courageous witness to the power of Jesus' resurrection.

Psalmist Preparation

In singing this responsorial psalm you not only celebrate deliverance from death but also accept the mission of proclaiming what God has done. The apostles accepted this mission knowing full well what it would cost (first reading). What is the cost to you? What is the reward?

Prayer

God of the resurrection, you continually raise us to new life from the destructiveness of our fears and infidelities. Help us witness to others the graciousness of your restoration that they, too, may come to new life in you. We ask this through Christ our Lord. Amen.

Gospel (John 10:27-30; L51C)

Jesus said: "My sheep hear my voice; I know them, and
they follow me. I give them eternal life, and they shall
never perish. No one can take them out of my hand.
My Father, who has given them to me, is greater
than all, and no one can take them out of the
Father's hand. The Father and I are one."

First Reading (Acts 13:14, 43-52)

Paul and Barnabas continued on from Perga and
reached Antioch in Pisidia. On the sabbath they
entered the synagogue and took their seats. Many Jews and worshipers
who were converts to Judaism followed Paul and Barnabas, who spoke to
them and urged them to remain faithful to the grace of God.

On the following sabbath almost the whole city gathered to hear the
word of the Lord. When the Jews saw the crowds, they were filled with
jealousy and with violent abuse contradicted what Paul said. Both Paul
and Barnabas spoke out boldly and said, "It was necessary that the word
of God be spoken to you first, but since you reject it and condemn yourselves as unworthy of eternal life, we now turn to the Gentiles. For so the
Lord has commanded us, *I have made you a light to the Gentiles, that you
may be an instrument of salvation to the ends of the earth.*"

The Gentiles were delighted when they heard this and glorified the
word of the Lord. All who were destined for eternal life came to believe,
and the word of the Lord continued to spread through the whole region.
The Jews, however, incited the women of prominence who were worshipers and the leading men of the city, stirred up a persecution against Paul
and Barnabas, and expelled them from their territory. So they shook the
dust from their feet in protest against them, and went to Iconium. The
disciples were filled with joy and the Holy Spirit.

Responsorial Psalm (Ps 100:1-2, 3, 5)

℞. (3c) We are his people, the sheep of his flock. *or:* ℞. Alleluia.

Sing joyfully to the LORD, all you lands;
   serve the LORD with gladness;
   come before him with joyful song.

℞. We are his people, the sheep of his flock. *or:* ℞. Alleluia.

Know that the Lord is God;
   he made us, his we are;
   his people, the flock he tends.

R︶. We are his people, the sheep of his flock. *or:* R︶. Alleluia.

The Lord is good:
   his kindness endures forever,
   and his faithfulness, to all generations.

R︶. We are his people, the sheep of his flock. *or:* R︶. Alleluia.

See Appendix, p. 214, for Second Reading

Reflecting on Living the Gospel

Gift-giving creates memories of goodness, establishes a habit of self-giving, assures the gift-giver of sharing in the dignity of the receiver. The focus of this gospel is giving, giving, giving. The Father gives us to Jesus as his flock. We give Jesus our attentive listening and faithful following. Jesus gives us eternal Life. There are no qualifying words in this gospel at all, no "ifs" about the giving. This is simply the way living risen Life is.

Connecting the Responsorial Psalm to the Readings

Psalm 100 is part of a set of psalms (Pss 93; 95–100) which celebrate God's sovereignty over all things. Peoples of the ancient Near East acclaimed a god powerful because of specific acts, the greatest of which was creation. The Israelites believed that God acted not only to create the world but also to create them as a people. All forces inimical to Israel as a community—from natural disasters to human enemies—quelled before the power of God, who arranged all events in the cosmos to support their coming together as a people.

   In Christ God showed the ultimate creative power by overcoming death with resurrection. Out of this act God formed a new people beyond the boundaries of the community of Israel (first reading), a people "which no one could count, / from every nation, race, people, and tongue" (second reading). No powers of hell or destruction will prevail against this people, for it is God who leads and shepherds them (second reading, gospel). In singing Psalm 100 we proclaim who we are because of

Christ's death and resurrection: a people created by God, protected by God, and called by God to eternal life.

Psalmist Preparation

The Israelites understood that God created them as a people and continually shepherded them. So, too, does the church recognize that she is created and shepherded by God. How have you experienced God's shepherding love for the church? How has God shepherded you as an individual disciple? In what way(s) does the church particularly need God's shepherding care today? In what way(s) do you?

Prayer

Redeeming God, we are a people created by you, protected by you, and shepherded by you to eternal life. Lead us always to hear your voice, heed its call, and follow in the direction you have set for us. We ask this through Christ our Lord. Amen.

Gospel (John 13:31-33a, 34-35; L54C)

When Judas had left them, Jesus said, "Now is the Son of Man glorified, and God is glorified in him. If God is glorified in him, God will also glorify him in himself, and God will glorify him at once. My children, I will be with you only a little while longer. I give you a new commandment: love one another. As I have loved you, so you also should love one another. This is how all will know that you are my disciples, if you have love for one another."

First Reading (Acts 14:21-27)

After Paul and Barnabas had proclaimed the good news to that city and made a considerable number of disciples, they returned to Lystra and to Iconium and to Antioch. They strengthened the spirits of the disciples and exhorted them to persevere in the faith, saying, "It is necessary for us to undergo many hardships to enter the kingdom of God." They appointed elders for them in each church and, with prayer and fasting, commended them to the Lord in whom they had put their faith. Then they traveled through Pisidia and reached Pamphylia. After proclaiming the word at Perga they went down to Attalia. From there they sailed to Antioch, where they had been commended to the grace of God for the work they had now accomplished. And when they arrived, they called the church together and reported what God had done with them and how he had opened the door of faith to the Gentiles.

Responsorial Psalm (Ps 145:8-9, 10-11, 12-13)

R℣. (cf. 1) I will praise your name forever, my king and my God.
or: R℣. Alleluia.

The Lord is gracious and merciful,
    slow to anger and of great kindness.
The Lord is good to all
    and compassionate toward all his works.

R℣. I will praise your name forever, my king and my God. or: R℣. Alleluia.

Let all your works give you thanks, O Lord,
    and let your faithful ones bless you.

Let them discourse of the glory of your kingdom
    and speak of your might.

R⁊. I will praise your name forever, my king and my God. *or:* R⁊. Alleluia.

Let them make known your might to the children of Adam,
    and the glorious splendor of your kingdom.
Your kingdom is a kingdom for all ages,
    and your dominion endures through all generations.

R⁊. I will praise your name forever, my king and my God. *or:* R⁊. Alleluia.

See Appendix, p. 214, for Second Reading

Reflecting on Living the Gospel

Judas's departure initiates the events of Jesus' passion, death, and resurrection. Jesus' imminent departure initiates his giving the disciples the commandment to love as he has loved. Jesus' passion and death is the full revelation to us of what it means to love as Jesus loved. His resurrection is the full revelation of God's glory. Love means giving one's life for others. This is God's glory. This is Jesus' glory. This is our glory.

Connecting the Responsorial Psalm to the Readings

In this responsorial psalm we call God to let divine works reveal the splendor of God's kingdom "for all ages." This kingdom is governed by God with graciousness, mercy, kindness, and compassion (psalm). This kingdom is the Good News Paul and Barnabas successfully preach to the Gentiles (first reading). This kingdom is the new heaven and new earth envisioned by John (second reading). In this kingdom we love one another as Jesus has loved us (gospel). We are capable of loving in this way because of the work of God in us, who has re-created us and chooses to dwell with us (second reading). When we let God do this work in us, we praise God's name, we reveal the glory of God's kingdom, we become God's greatest work.

Psalmist Preparation

Your singing of this responsorial psalm needs to invite the assembly to see themselves as a work of God, a new creation, giving praise. What might you do this week to help yourself see them in this way? to see yourself in this way? How is this way of seeing a living out of Jesus' commandment to love one another as he has loved us?

Prayer

God of love, in the life, death, and resurrection of your Son you have shown us the fullness of your love for us. Open our hearts that we may show this same love to one another and so complete your work of redemption. We ask this in his name. Amen.

Gospel (John 14:23-29; L57C)

Jesus said to his disciples: "Whoever loves me will keep my word, and my Father will love him, and we will come to him and make our dwelling with him. Whoever does not love me does not keep my words; yet the word you hear is not mine but that of the Father who sent me.

"I have told you this while I am with you. The Advocate, the Holy Spirit, whom the Father will send in my name, will teach you everything and remind you of all that I told you. Peace I leave with you; my peace I give to you. Not as the world gives do I give it to you. Do not let your hearts be troubled or afraid. You heard me tell you, 'I am going away and I will come back to you.' If you loved me, you would rejoice that I am going to the Father; for the Father is greater than I. And now I have told you this before it happens, so that when it happens you may believe."

First Reading (Acts 15:1-2, 22-29)

Some who had come down from Judea were instructing the brothers, "Unless you are circumcised according to the Mosaic practice, you cannot be saved." Because there arose no little dissension and debate by Paul and Barnabas with them, it was decided that Paul, Barnabas, and some of the others should go up to Jerusalem to the apostles and elders about this question.

The apostles and elders, in agreement with the whole church, decided to choose representatives and to send them to Antioch with Paul and Barnabas. The ones chosen were Judas, who was called Barsabbas, and Silas, leaders among the brothers. This is the letter delivered by them: "The apostles and the elders, your brothers, to the brothers in Antioch, Syria, and Cilicia of Gentile origin: greetings. Since we have heard that some of our number who went out without any mandate from us have upset you with their teachings and disturbed your peace of mind, we have with one accord decided to choose representatives and to send them to you along with our beloved Barnabas and Paul, who have dedicated their lives to the name of our Lord Jesus Christ. So we are sending Judas and Silas who will also convey this same message by word of mouth: 'It is the decision of the Holy Spirit and of us not to place on you any burden beyond these necessities, namely, to abstain from meat sacrificed to idols, from blood, from meats of strangled animals, and from unlawful marriage. If you keep free of these, you will be doing what is right. Farewell.'"

Responsorial Psalm (Ps 67:2-3, 5, 6, 8)

(R℣. 4) O God, let all the nations praise you! *or:* R℣. Alleluia.

May God have pity on us and bless us;
   may he let his face shine upon us.
So may your way be known upon earth;
   among all nations, your salvation.

R℣. O God, let all the nations praise you! *or:* R℣. Alleluia.

May the nations be glad and exult
   because you rule the peoples in equity;
   the nations on the earth you guide.

R℣. O God, let all the nations praise you! *or:* R℣. Alleluia.

May the peoples praise you, O God;
   may all the peoples praise you!
May God bless us,
   and may all the ends of the earth fear him!

R℣. O God, let all the nations praise you! *or:* R℣. Alleluia.

See Appendix, p. 215, for Second Reading

Reflecting on Living the Gospel

The word of Jesus we are to keep is his command to love as he loves us. Jesus' word, however, is not simply spoken, but is love-in-action. His love-in-action is the gift of the Spirit of peace, of untroubled hearts, of rejoicing, of believing. His love-in-action is ultimately the gift of the resurrection. Our love-in-action flows from the gift of the Holy Spirit dwelling in us and teaching us to keep Jesus' word-command to love. Our love-in-action is risen Life-made-visible.

Connecting the Responsorial Psalm to the Readings

Psalm 67 was a hymn of thanksgiving for a fruitful harvest. The Israelites prayed that God would extend these abundant blessings to all the earth. In this way all nations would know God's saving care and offer joyful praise. In the context of today's readings, Psalm 67 invites us to make our very way of living the abundant harvest God offers the world.

When we love Jesus and keep his word, we move beyond the temptation to limit God's presence and power to specific practices (first reading) and places (second reading). We become the very dwelling place of God on earth (gospel). Let us pray together that our manner of living and relating will make God's way "known upon earth" (psalm) and that through us all nations will come to know salvation.

Psalmist Preparation

The harvest for which you praise God in this responsorial psalm is the salvation wrought through the death and resurrection of Christ. You pray that all nations will come to know this salvation. Who has helped you come to know and believe in it? To whom are you making it known?

Prayer

God of life, you come to us in love and make your dwelling within us. Lead us to believe in your presence, to heed your word, and to proclaim your love to all nations. We ask this through Christ our Lord. Amen.

Gospel (Luke 24:46-53; L58C)

Jesus said to his disciples: "Thus it is written that the Christ would suffer and rise from the dead on the third day and that repentance, for the forgiveness of sins, would be preached in his name to all the nations, beginning from Jerusalem. You are witnesses of these things. And behold I am sending the promise of my Father upon you; but stay in the city until you are clothed with power from on high."

Then he led them out as far as Bethany, raised his hands, and blessed them. As he blessed them he parted from them and was taken up to heaven. They did him homage and then returned to Jerusalem with great joy, and they were continually in the temple praising God.

First Reading (Acts 1:1-11)

In the first book, Theophilus, I dealt with all that Jesus did and taught until the day he was taken up, after giving instructions through the Holy Spirit to the apostles whom he had chosen. He presented himself alive to them by many proofs after he had suffered, appearing to them during forty days and speaking about the kingdom of God. While meeting with them, he enjoined them not to depart from Jerusalem, but to wait for "the promise of the Father about which you have heard me speak; for John baptized with water, but in a few days you will be baptized with the Holy Spirit."

When they had gathered together they asked him, "Lord, are you at this time going to restore the kingdom to Israel?" He answered them, "It is not for you to know the times or seasons that the Father has established by his own authority. But you will receive power when the Holy Spirit comes upon you, and you will be my witnesses in Jerusalem, throughout Judea and Samaria, and to the ends of the earth." When he had said this, as they were looking on, he was lifted up, and a cloud took him from their sight. While they were looking intently at the sky as he was going, suddenly two men dressed in white garments stood beside them. They said, "Men of Galilee, why are you standing there looking at the sky? This Jesus who has been taken up from you into heaven will return in the same way as you have seen him going into heaven."

Responsorial Psalm (Ps 47:2-3, 6-7, 8-9)

R℣. (6) God mounts his throne to shouts of joy: a blare of trumpets for the Lord. *or:* R℣. Alleluia.

All you peoples, clap your hands,
    shout to God with cries of gladness,
for the LORD, the Most High, the awesome,
    is the great king over all the earth.

R℣. God mounts his throne to shouts of joy: a blare of trumpets for the Lord. *or:* R℣. Alleluia.

God mounts his throne amid shouts of joy;
    the LORD, amid trumpet blasts.
Sing praise to God, sing praise;
    sing praise to our king, sing praise.

R℣. God mounts his throne to shouts of joy: a blare of trumpets for the Lord. *or:* R℣. Alleluia.

For king of all the earth is God;
    sing hymns of praise.
God reigns over the nations,
    God sits upon his holy throne.

R℣. God mounts his throne to shouts of joy: a blare of trumpets for the Lord. *or:* R℣. Alleluia.

See Appendix, p. 215, for Second Reading

Reflecting on Living the Gospel

Jesus' ascension, for us, is a gift and commissioning. We receive the gift of the Holy Spirit. We preach and teach in his name. We don't do this on our own, as Jesus promised. We can't set out to take up Jesus' mission to preach the Good News until we open ourselves to the Holy Spirit's Presence with and among us. This ensures us that our work isn't ours but Christ's. Ultimately our mission is to preach not simply events but a Person—Jesus Christ, the risen One.

Connecting the Responsorial Psalm to the Readings

Psalm 47 was an enthronement psalm used when the ark of the covenant was carried in procession into the temple. It celebrated God's sovereignty over all heaven and earth. The song contains verses (omitted from this responsorial psalm) that express Israel's belief that God chose them to play a special role in establishing God's reign over all nations.

Knowing the full text of this psalm brings its use on this solemnity into fuller perspective. The psalm is not just about the historical ascension of Jesus to the throne of God but includes our participation in his ascendancy. We, too, "have confidence of entrance into the sanctuary" (second reading). Though we do not know the time of the kingdom's coming, we do witness to its presence (first reading). We have been blessed by Christ to tell of it (gospel). By Jesus' ascension all humanity is raised to the glory of God. When we sing Psalm 47 on this solemnity, this is what we witness to, celebrate, and proclaim.

Psalmist Preparation

On the surface you can interpret this psalm as a celebration of the historical event of Jesus' ascension. But it is about far more than that. The psalm is about the complete victory of the whole Body of Christ over the forces of sin and death. Who sits on the "holy throne"? You do. The assembly does. The church does. As you prepare to sing this psalm, you need to reflect on this fuller understanding so that you can move the assembly, and yourself, from historicizing about Jesus' life and mission to personally participating in it.

Prayer

God of glory, you raised us with your Son to be seated at your right hand. With him, we are victors over sin and death. With him, we sing your praises forever. Lead us, with him, to give our lives that all peoples may know the dignity to which you have called them. We ask this through him, the risen One who sits at your right hand in glory. Amen.

Gospel (John 17:20-26; L61C)

Lifting up his eyes to heaven, Jesus prayed, saying: "Holy Father, I pray not only for them, but also for those who will believe in me through their word, so that they may all be one, as you, Father, are in me and I in you, that they also may be in us, that the world may believe that you sent me. And I have given them the glory you gave me, so that they may be one, as we are one, I in them and you in me, that they may be brought to perfection as one, that the world may know that you sent me, and that you loved them even as you loved me. Father, they are your gift to me. I wish that where I am they also may be with me, that they may see my glory that you gave me, because you loved me before the foundation of the world. Righteous Father, the world also does not know you, but I know you, and they know that you sent me. I made known to them your name and I will make it known, that the love with which you loved me may be in them and I in them."

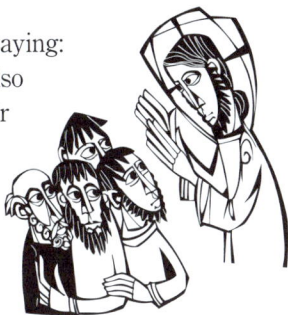

First Reading (Acts 7:55-60)

Stephen, filled with the Holy Spirit, looked up intently to heaven and saw the glory of God and Jesus standing at the right hand of God, and Stephen said, "Behold, I see the heavens opened and the Son of Man standing at the right hand of God." But they cried out in a loud voice, covered their ears, and rushed upon him together. They threw him out of the city, and began to stone him. The witnesses laid down their cloaks at the feet of a young man named Saul. As they were stoning Stephen, he called out, "Lord Jesus, receive my spirit." Then he fell to his knees and cried out in a loud voice, "Lord, do not hold this sin against them"; and when he said this, he fell asleep.

Responsorial Psalm (Ps 97:1-2, 6-7, 9)

℟. (1a and 9a) The Lord is king, the most high over all the earth.
or: ℟. Alleluia.

The LORD is king; let the earth rejoice;
    let the many islands be glad.
Justice and judgment are the foundation of his throne.

℟. The Lord is king, the most high over all the earth. *or:* ℟. Alleluia.

The heavens proclaim his justice,
　and all peoples see his glory.
All gods are prostrate before him.

R℣. The Lord is king, the most high over all the earth. *or:* R℣. Alleluia.

You, O Lᴏʀᴅ, are the Most High over all the earth,
　exalted far above all gods.

R℣. The Lord is king, the most high over all the earth. *or:* R℣. Alleluia.

See Appendix, p. 215, for Second Reading

Reflecting on Living the Gospel

Jesus' prayer for his disciples at the Last Supper is not only for them, "but also for those who will believe in" him because they have heard the disciples' word. This includes each one of us, here and now. His prayer for us? That we "be one" in him, that we share in Jesus' risen glory, that we "be brought to perfection," that we be loved, that we know Jesus was sent by the Father. Our work: to transform the world.

Connecting the Responsorial Psalm to the Readings

Psalm 97 is a hymn celebrating God's sovereignty over all that exists. The verses used here retell the vision that strengthens Stephen to remain steadfast in discipleship to the point of death (first reading). Stephen sees the glory of God in heaven and Jesus standing at God's right hand and proclaims what he sees to the people surrounding him. Even more, he dies as Jesus did, giving himself over to God and forgiving those who have murdered him. In return he is raised to the glory of eternal life (second reading). We sing these psalm verses because we have been granted the same vision as Stephen and we have been called to the same discipleship. In singing this psalm we acclaim that we, too, have seen the glory of Jesus and that we, too, will stake our lives on it.

Psalmist Preparation

Because Psalm 97 is a generic text about the glory of God, it would be easy to sing it in a perfunctory way. But the context of Stephen's martyrdom (first reading) and Jesus' prayer that his disciples be one with him and the Father (gospel) invite a much deeper interpretation. To see the glory of God means to discover the mystery of your own glory. To become one with Christ means to accept that such glorification can come only through death. To sing these verses means to lay down your life in surrender and belief as did Stephen. This, then, is no simple song. Are you willing to sing it?

Prayer
God of power and might, you sent your Son to reveal that you dwell not only in the heavens but also in our hearts. In him we have been consecrated to your truth. Keep us faithful to this consecration and send us forth with courage and power to be his redeeming presence in the world. We ask this in his name. Amen.

Gospel (John 14:15-16, 23b-26; L63C)

Jesus said to his disciples: "If you love me, you will keep my commandments. And I will ask the Father, and he will give you another Advocate to be with you always.

"Whoever loves me will keep my word, and my Father will love him, and we will come to him and make our dwelling with him. Those who do not love me do not keep my words; yet the word you hear is not mine but that of the Father who sent me.

"I have told you this while I am with you. The Advocate, the Holy Spirit whom the Father will send in my name, will teach you everything and remind you of all that I told you."

or Gospel (John 20:19-23; L63C)

First Reading (Acts 2:1-11)

When the time for Pentecost was fulfilled, they were all in one place together. And suddenly there came from the sky a noise like a strong driving wind, and it filled the entire house in which they were. Then there appeared to them tongues as of fire, which parted and came to rest on each one of them. And they were all filled with the Holy Spirit and began to speak in different tongues, as the Spirit enabled them to proclaim.

Now there were devout Jews from every nation under heaven staying in Jerusalem. At this sound, they gathered in a large crowd, but they were confused because each one heard them speaking in his own language. They were astounded, and in amazement they asked, "Are not all these people who are speaking Galileans? Then how does each of us hear them in his native language? We are Parthians, Medes, and Elamites, inhabitants of Mesopotamia, Judea and Cappadocia, Pontus and Asia, Phrygia and Pamphylia, Egypt and the districts of Libya near Cyrene, as well as travelers from Rome, both Jews and converts to Judaism, Cretans and Arabs, yet we hear them speaking in our own tongues of the mighty acts of God."

Responsorial Psalm (Ps 104:1, 24, 29-30, 31, 34)

R̢. (cf. 30) Lord, send out your Spirit, and renew the face of the earth.
or: R̢. Alleluia.

Bless the LORD, O my soul!
    O LORD, my God, you are great indeed!

How manifold are your works, O Lᴏʀᴅ!
The earth is full of your creatures.

Rℐ. Lord, send out your Spirit, and renew the face of the earth.
or: Rℐ. Alleluia.

If you take away their breath, they perish
and return to their dust.
When you send forth your spirit, they are created,
and you renew the face of the earth.

Rℐ. Lord, send out your Spirit, and renew the face of the earth.
or: Rℐ. Alleluia.

May the glory of the Lᴏʀᴅ endure forever;
may the Lᴏʀᴅ be glad in his works!
Pleasing to him be my theme;
I will be glad in the Lᴏʀᴅ.

Rℐ. Lord, send out your Spirit, and renew the face of the earth.
or: Rℐ. Alleluia.

See Appendix, p. 216, for Second Reading

Reflecting on Living the Gospel
The Father sent the "Advocate, the Holy Spirit" to teach us "everything."
What is this "everything" we need the Spirit to teach us? Why and how
keeping Jesus' commandments and word is the unconditional condition
of loving him. Why and how this love is the wellspring of our relationship to Jesus and his Father in their Spirit. What the Spirit teaches us, in
the end, is why we do anything and how we do everything. Oh, how we
need Pentecost!

Connecting the Responsorial Psalm to the Readings
Psalm 104 is a masterful hymn praising God for the creation of the cosmos. It unfolds in a seven-part structure paralleling the creation account
in Genesis 1. The Hebrews believed the cause of creation to be God's
breath or spirit (*ruach*). Take divine breath away and creatures would
die; give them breath/spirit and they would live (vv. 29-30).

In the first reading this breath of God comes like a "strong driving
wind," which enables the disciples to witness to "the mighty acts of
God." In the second reading this breath comes as a "Spirit of adoption,"

making us sons and daughters of God. In the gospel this breath comes as Advocate sent in Jesus' name to teach us all things. This is the Spirit we ask God to send us in the responsorial psalm: the power pushing us forward in mission, the love which is God's very life within us, and the spokesperson reminding us of all that Jesus has taught—truly a Breath that will re-create the universe!

Psalmist Preparation

You pray in this responsorial psalm for the renewal of the church—the renewal of her knowledge of Christ (gospel), the renewal of her sense of identity as one body (second reading), and the renewal of her commitment to mission (first reading). How have these weeks of Easter renewed you as a member of the church?

Prayer

Creating God, you continually send your Spirit to renew our relationships through the power of forgiveness. Open our hearts to hear what the Spirit teaches and strengthen our wills to do as the Spirit directs, that the face of the earth may be renewed. We ask this through Christ our Lord. Amen

Gospel (John 16:12-15; L166C)

Jesus said to his disciples: "I have much more to tell you, but you cannot bear it now. But when he comes, the Spirit of truth, he will guide you to all truth. He will not speak on his own, but he will speak what he hears, and will declare to you the things that are coming. He will glorify me, because he will take from what is mine and declare it to you. Everything that the Father has is mine; for this reason I told you that he will take from what is mine and declare it to you."

First Reading (Prov 8:22-31)

Thus says the wisdom of God:
"The LORD possessed me, the beginning of his ways,
    the forerunner of his prodigies of long ago;
from of old I was poured forth,
    at the first, before the earth.
When there were no depths I was brought forth,
    when there were no fountains or springs of water;
before the mountains were settled into place,
    before the hills, I was brought forth;
while as yet the earth and fields were not made,
    nor the first clods of the world.

"When the Lord established the heavens I was there,
    when he marked out the vault over the face of the deep;
when he made firm the skies above,
    when he fixed fast the foundations of the earth;
when he set for the sea its limit,
    so that the waters should not transgress his command;
then was I beside him as his craftsman,
    and I was his delight day by day,
playing before him all the while,
    playing on the surface of his earth;
    and I found delight in the human race."

Responsorial Psalm (Ps 8:4-5, 6-7, 8-9)

℟. O Lord, our God, how wonderful your name in all the earth!

When I behold your heavens, the work of your fingers,
　　the moon and the stars which you set in place—
what is man that you should be mindful of him,
　　or the son of man that you should care for him?

℟. O Lord, our God, how wonderful your name in all the earth!

You have made him little less than the angels,
　　and crowned him with glory and honor.
You have given him rule over the works of your hands,
　　putting all things under his feet.

℟. O Lord, our God, how wonderful your name in all the earth!

All sheep and oxen,
　　yes, and the beasts of the field,
the birds of the air, the fishes of the sea,
　　and whatever swims the paths of the seas.

℟. O Lord, our God, how wonderful your name in all the earth!

See Appendix, p. 216, for Second Reading

Reflecting on Living the Gospel

The Father gives everything to Jesus; the Spirit takes from Jesus to "declare to [us] the things that are coming." Give and take. Such is the dynamic of the inner Life of the Trinity. Such is the dynamic of how the Father, Jesus, and the Spirit engage us in their Life. Give and take. We can "bear" the "much more" the Spirit has to tell us when we surrender more fully to the trinitarian Life within us. Give and take.

Connecting the Responsorial Psalm to the Readings

The responsorial psalm for this solemnity of the Trinity asks who we are in the eyes of God. The readings for this Sunday reveal the high value God places on us human beings. In the first reading the wisdom of God "play[s] on the surface of his earth" and "[finds] delight in the human race." In the second reading God pours God's own love into our hearts through the gift of the Holy Spirit. In the gospel Jesus promises that the Spirit will give to us everything that belongs to him and the Father. Truly God has "made [us] little less than the angels" and has "crowned [us] with glory and honor" (psalm). In singing this psalm we acknowledge the greatness of the Trinity who gives all so that we might become more.

Psalmist Preparation

This responsorial psalm is not so much about our greatness as human beings as about the beneficence of God, who treats us with unimaginable dignity and grace. How this week might you treat those whom you meet with this same dignity and grace—at home? at work? on the street?

Prayer

Triune God, you grant us unimaginable dignity and grace by creating us in your own image. Lead us to live as your sons and daughters who dance with creation and delight in one another. We ask this through Christ our Lord. Amen.

Gospel (Luke 9:11b-17; L169C)

Jesus spoke to the crowds about the kingdom of God, and he healed those who needed to be cured. As the day was drawing to a close, the Twelve approached him and said, "Dismiss the crowd so that they can go to the surrounding villages and farms and find lodging and provisions; for we are in a deserted place here." He said to them, "Give them some food yourselves." They replied, "Five loaves and two fish are all we have, unless we ourselves go and buy food for all these people." Now the men there numbered about five thousand. Then he said to his disciples, "Have them sit down in groups of about fifty." They did so and made them all sit down. Then taking the five loaves and the two fish, and looking up to heaven, he said the blessing over them, broke them, and gave them to the disciples to set before the crowd. They all ate and were satisfied. And when the leftover fragments were picked up, they filled twelve wicker baskets.

First Reading (Gen 14:18-20)

In those days, Melchizedek, king of Salem, brought out bread and wine, and being a priest of God Most High, he blessed Abram with these words:

"Blessed be Abram by God Most High,
the creator of heaven and earth;
and blessed be God Most High,
who delivered your foes into your hand."

Then Abram gave him a tenth of everything.

Responsorial Psalm (Ps 110:1, 2, 3, 4)

R̴. (4b) You are a priest forever, in the line of Melchizedek.

The LORD said to my Lord: "Sit at my right hand
till I make your enemies your footstool."

R̴. You are a priest forever, in the line of Melchizedek.

The scepter of your power the LORD will stretch forth from Zion:
"Rule in the midst of your enemies."

R̴. You are a priest forever, in the line of Melchizedek.

"Yours is princely power in the day of your birth, in holy splendor;
   before the daystar, like the dew, I have begotten you."

℞. You are a priest forever, in the line of Melchizedek.

The LORD has sworn, and he will not repent:
   "You are a priest forever, according to the order of Melchizedek."

℞. You are a priest forever, in the line of Melchizedek.

See Appendix, p. 216, for Second Reading

Reflecting on Living the Gospel

Jesus does far more than satisfy physical hunger; he foreshadows the gift
of his very self as the Bread of Life. Jesus taught the crowds and
"healed those who needed to be cured." Our need for Jesus and what he
gives us, however, goes beyond teaching and healing. Even more, we
need the food Jesus gives in unfathomable abundance. This food transforms us into being the "leftover fragments"—the Body of Christ—continuing Jesus' ministry of giving self over for others.

Connecting the Responsorial Psalm to the Readings

Psalm 110 was a royal psalm used at the coronation ceremony of a king
descended from the line of David. The text promised the king a place of
honor next to God, victory over enemies, and a priestly role before the
people. In the first reading Melchizedek, "a priest of God Most High"
gives food, drink, and blessing to Abram. In the gospel Jesus heals those
in need and feeds the starving crowd, creating an amazing abundance
out of a meager supply. In the second reading Paul reminds us that the
food and drink Jesus gives us is his very Body and Blood. In singing this
psalm we recognize what Jesus does and who Jesus is. He is the one vic-
torious over all that impedes fullness of life. He is the one who feeds us
with his very self. He is the completion of the Davidic line and a "priest
forever, in the line of Melchizedek."

Psalmist Preparation

The psalm you sing this Sunday acclaims the power and priesthood of
Christ, both most evident to us in the gift of his Body and Blood for food.
What might you do this week to affirm your personal faith in Jesus and
express your gratitude for what he does in giving us the Eucharist?

THE MOST HOLY BODY AND BLOOD OF CHRIST (CORPUS CHRISTI)

Prayer

Nourishing God, in the gift of your Son you feed us with the best of wheat and fill us with abundant life. May our feasting on his Body and Blood strengthen us to hand over our bodies as nourishment for others. We ask this in his name. Amen.

Gospel (Luke 7:11-17; L90C)

Jesus journeyed to a city called Nain, and his disciples and a large crowd accompanied him. As he drew near to the gate of the city, a man who had died was being carried out, the only son of his mother, and she was a widow. A large crowd from the city was with her. When the Lord saw her, he was moved with pity for her and said to her, "Do not weep." He stepped forward and touched the coffin; at this the bearers halted, and he said, "Young man, I tell you, arise!" The dead man sat up and began to speak, and Jesus gave him to his mother. Fear seized them all, and they glorified God, exclaiming, "A great prophet has arisen in our midst," and "God has visited his people." This report about him spread through the whole of Judea and in all the surrounding region.

First Reading (1 Kgs 17:17-24)

Elijah went to Zarephath of Sidon to the house of a widow.
The son of the mistress of the house fell sick,
    and his sickness grew more severe until he stopped breathing.
So she said to Elijah,
    "Why have you done this to me, O man of God?
Have you come to me to call attention to my guilt
    and to kill my son?"
Elijah said to her, "Give me your son."
Taking him from her lap, he carried the son to the upper room
    where he was staying, and put him on his bed.
Elijah called out to the LORD:
    "O LORD, my God,
    will you afflict even the widow with whom I am staying
    by killing her son?"
Then he stretched himself out upon the child three times
    and called out to the LORD:
    "O LORD, my God,
    let the life breath return to the body of this child."

TENTH SUNDAY IN ORDINARY TIME

The Lord heard the prayer of Elijah;
   the life breath returned to the child's body and he revived.
Taking the child, Elijah brought him down into the house
   from the upper room and gave him to his mother.
Elijah said to her, "See! Your son is alive."
The woman replied to Elijah,
   "Now indeed I know that you are a man of God.
The word of the Lord comes truly from your mouth."

Responsorial Psalm (Ps 30:2, 4, 5-6, 11, 12, 13)

℟. (2a) I will praise you, Lord, for you have rescued me.

I will extol you, O Lord, for you drew me clear
   and did not let my enemies rejoice over me.
O Lord, you brought me up from the nether world;
   you preserved me from among those going down into the pit.

℟. I will praise you, Lord, for you have rescued me.

Sing praise to the Lord, you his faithful ones,
   and give thanks to his holy name.
For his anger lasts but a moment;
   a lifetime, his good will.
At nightfall, weeping enters in,
   but with the dawn, rejoicing.

℟. I will praise you, Lord, for you have rescued me.

Hear, O Lord, and have pity on me;
   O Lord, be my helper.
You changed my mourning into dancing;
   O Lord, my God, forever will I give you thanks.

℟. I will praise you, Lord, for you have rescued me.

Second Reading (Gal 1:11-19)

Reflecting on Living the Gospel

The widow of Nain had lost everything dear to her: her husband and her only son. In them she had lost her life support and any hope of posterity. Without even being asked, Jesus with great compassion raises her son from the dead and gives him back to her. By word and deed Jesus restores the widow's life and hope. In Jesus "God has visited his people." In Jesus God continues to visit us, offering hope and life, even without our asking. Do we accept?

Connecting the Responsorial Psalm to the Readings

The Sunday Lectionary uses Psalm 30 four times (Easter Vigil 4, Third Sunday of Easter C, Tenth Sunday in Ordinary Time C, and Thirteenth Sunday in Ordinary Time B) and every time the readings deal with our need to be delivered from death. Even though God has made all things for life, we nonetheless experience death coming toward us over and over, bringing pain, grief, and even guilt (first reading). The stories of two grieving widows, however, show us God acting to change our weeping into rejoicing, our mourning into dancing (psalm). In the first reading, God restores life through the prayer of a faithful prophet. In the gospel, God restores life through the words and actions of Christ, who holds power over death. These verses from Psalm 30 acknowledge what oftentimes only our faith can see: that death with its contingent weeping and mourning is not the end of the story—life is.

Psalmist Preparation

When you sing this psalm, you embody the confidence of the entire Body of Christ that God saves from death, even when the whole world groans under its threat. Pray this week for those who are facing death in any form—physical, mental, emotional. Pray that your singing may be a song of hope for them.

Prayer

God of salvation, we thank you for the gift of your Son, Jesus, in whom all human weeping becomes rejoicing and all death becomes a doorway to new life. In him may we walk joyfully toward the fullness of life. We ask this in his name. Amen.

***Gospel* (Luke 7:36–8:3**
[or Luke 7:36-50]; L93C)

A Pharisee invited Jesus to dine with him, and he entered the Pharisee's house and reclined at table. Now
there was a sinful woman in the city who learned that
he was at table in the house of the Pharisee. Bringing an
alabaster flask of ointment, she stood behind him at
his feet weeping and began to bathe his feet with
her tears. Then she wiped them with her hair,
kissed them, and anointed them with the
ointment. When the Pharisee who had invited him saw this he said to himself, "If this
man were a prophet, he would know who and
what sort of woman this is who is touching him, that she is a sinner."
Jesus said to him in reply, "Simon, I have something to say to you." "Tell
me, teacher," he said. "Two people were in debt to a certain creditor; one
owed five hundred days' wages and the other owed fifty. Since they were
unable to repay the debt, he forgave it for both. Which of them will love
him more?" Simon said in reply, "The one, I suppose, whose larger debt
was forgiven." He said to him, "You have judged rightly."

Then he turned to the woman and said to Simon, "Do you see this
woman? When I entered your house, you did not give me water for my
feet, but she has bathed them with her tears and wiped them with her
hair. You did not give me a kiss, but she has not ceased kissing my feet
since the time I entered. You did not anoint my head with oil, but she
anointed my feet with ointment. So I tell you, her many sins have been
forgiven because she has shown great love. But the one to whom little is
forgiven, loves little." He said to her, "Your sins are forgiven." The others
at table said to themselves, "Who is this who even forgives sins?" But he
said to the woman, "Your faith has saved you; go in peace."

Afterward he journeyed from one town and village to another, preach-
ing and proclaiming the good news of the kingdom of God. Accompany-
ing him were the Twelve and some women who had been cured of evil
spirits and infirmities, Mary, called Magdalene, from whom seven demons
had gone out, Joanna, the wife of Herod's steward Chuza, Susanna, and
many others who provided for them out of their resources.

First Reading (2 Sam 12:7-10, 13)

Nathan said to David: "Thus says the Lord God of Israel: 'I anointed you king of Israel. I rescued you from the hand of Saul. I gave you your lord's house and your lord's wives for your own. I gave you the house of Israel and of Judah. And if this were not enough, I could count up for you still more. Why have you spurned the Lord and done evil in his sight? You have cut down Uriah the Hittite with the sword; you took his wife as your own, and him you killed with the sword of the Ammonites. Now, therefore, the sword shall never depart from your house, because you have despised me and have taken the wife of Uriah to be your wife.'" Then David said to Nathan, "I have sinned against the Lord." Nathan answered David: "The Lord on his part has forgiven your sin: you shall not die."

Responsorial Psalm (Ps 32:1-2, 5, 7, 11)

R℣. (cf. 5c) Lord, forgive the wrong I have done.

Blessed is the one whose fault is taken away,
    whose sin is covered.
Blessed the man to whom the Lord imputes no guilt,
    in whose spirit there is no guile.

R℣. Lord, forgive the wrong I have done.

I acknowledged my sin to you,
    my guilt I covered not.
I said, "I confess my faults to the Lord,"
    and you took away the guilt of my sin.

R℣. Lord, forgive the wrong I have done.

You are my shelter; from distress you will preserve me;
    with glad cries of freedom you will ring me round.

R℣. Lord, forgive the wrong I have done.

Be glad in the Lord and rejoice, you just;
    exult, all you upright of heart.

R℣. Lord, forgive the wrong I have done.

Second Reading (Gal 2:16, 19-21)

Reflecting on Living the Gospel

This gospel depicts two very different ways of relating to Jesus. Simon the Pharisee related to Jesus as a one-time visitor, maintaining only a surface relationship having no power to transform him. The "sinful woman," on the other hand, related to Jesus as an intimate, avowing an underlying relationship that transformed her. How do we relate to Jesus? Do we wish to be intimate and close to Jesus, or do we keep a protective distance?

Connecting the Responsorial Psalm to the Readings

In this responsorial psalm the one praying relates a personal experience of having confessed sin and received divine mercy. The Lectionary omits verses 3-4 of Psalm 32, in which the person praying admits to having initially refused to accept his or her guilt, choosing instead to resist self-examination and honest confession. When the psalmist finally relents and confesses, God grants overwhelming forgiveness. The story of Psalm 32 is told dramatically in the confrontation between Nathan and David (first reading) and in the encounter between the sinful woman and Jesus (gospel). Moreover, it is told dramatically in our own lives every time we confess our wrongdoing. God forgives us and replaces our guilt with newfound freedom and joy (psalm).

Psalmist Preparation

Spend some time this week reflecting on the overwhelming mercy of God who longs to forgive no matter what the sin. What moves you to ask for this forgiveness? What moves you to resist it?

Prayer

Compassionate God, your mercy is without limit. Give us the courage to admit our sinfulness, turn toward you, and receive the new life your healing forgiveness offers. We ask this through Christ our Lord. Amen.

Gospel (Luke 9:18-24; L96C)

Once when Jesus was praying in solitude, and the disciples were with him, he asked them, "Who do the crowds say that I am?" They said in reply, "John the Baptist; others, Elijah; still others, 'One of the ancient prophets has arisen.'" Then he said to them, "But who do you say that I am?" Peter said in reply, "The Christ of God." He rebuked them and directed them not to tell this to anyone.

He said, "The Son of Man must suffer greatly and be rejected by the elders, the chief priests, and the scribes, and be killed and on the third day be raised." Then he said to all, "If anyone wishes to come after me, he must deny himself and take up his cross daily and follow me. For whoever wishes to save his life will lose it, but whoever loses his life for my sake will save it."

First Reading (Zech 12:10-11; 13:1)

Thus says the LORD: I will pour out on the house of David and on the inhabitants of Jerusalem a spirit of grace and petition; and they shall look on him whom they have pierced, and they shall mourn for him as one mourns for an only son, and they shall grieve over him as one grieves over a firstborn.

On that day the mourning in Jerusalem shall be as great as the mourning of Hadadrimmon in the plain of Megiddo.

On that day there shall be open to the house of David and to the inhabitants of Jerusalem, a fountain to purify from sin and uncleanness.

Responsorial Psalm (Ps 63:2, 3-4, 5-6, 8-9)

R̸. My soul is thirsting for you, O Lord my God.

O God, you are my God whom I seek;
    for you my flesh pines and my soul thirsts
    like the earth, parched, lifeless and without water.

R̸. My soul is thirsting for you, O Lord my God.

Thus have I gazed toward you in the sanctuary
  to see your power and your glory,
for your kindness is a greater good than life;
  my lips shall glorify you.

R̸. My soul is thirsting for you, O Lord my God.

Thus will I bless you while I live;
  lifting up my hands, I will call upon your name.
As with the riches of a banquet shall my soul be satisfied,
  and with exultant lips my mouth shall praise you.

R̸. My soul is thirsting for you, O Lord my God.

You are my help,
  and in the shadow of your wings I shout for joy.
My soul clings fast to you;
  your right hand upholds me.

R̸. My soul is thirsting for you, O Lord my God.

Second Reading (Gal 3:26-29)

Reflecting on Living the Gospel
It was out of his prayer that Jesus asked his disciples, "who do you say
that I am?" and revealed that his very identity entailed suffering, rejection, death, and resurrection. Our own prayer is to lead us to clearer
understanding of who we are, and to the revelation that our very identity
as disciples entails denying self, taking up our daily cross, and losing our
life for the sake of others. Dare we pray? Dare we ask Jesus, "who do *you*
say that *I* am?"

Connecting the Responsorial Psalm to the Readings
In the first reading God pours onto the people a "spirit of grace and petition." Their prayer moves them to acknowledge their sinfulness, mourn
what they have done, and receive purification. The gospel also relates a
moment of prayer out of which Jesus leads the disciples to acknowledge
who he is and to accept the suffering that he, and they with him, must
undergo.

The responsorial psalm reminds us that prayer—thirsting for God—
is the fountainhead of redemption. On the one hand, prayer is a gift from
God (first reading). On the other, it is a choice on our part. Always it is a
relationship that reveals both who God is and who we are. Prayer
teaches us that we are souls in need of divine nourishment (psalm), sin-

ners in need of repentance and purification (first reading), and disciples called to acknowledge Christ and carry the cross (gospel). Prayer also teaches us that God is our greatest good and ultimate satisfaction, that God acts to bring us to repentance, and that God in Christ takes up the cross ahead of us. May we know for whom we thirst, and may we drink deeply.

Psalmist Preparation

In the context of this Sunday's readings this responsorial psalm is a courageous prayer to make. Jesus pours out his thirst for God in his own prayer (gospel). You join Jesus in this prayer and in the choice it implies to accept suffering and death in order to follow Jesus. Are you willing to accept where thirsting for God will ultimately lead you?

Prayer

Redeeming God, you satisfy our every desire with the gift of your salvation. Lead us to thirst only for you and give us the courage to empty ourselves that we may be filled with your divine life. We ask this through Christ our Lord. Amen.

Gospel (Luke 9:51-62; L99C)

When the days for Jesus' being taken up were fulfilled, he resolutely determined to journey to Jerusalem, and he sent messengers ahead of him. On the way they entered a Samaritan village to prepare for his reception there, but they would not welcome him because the destination of his journey was Jerusalem.

When the disciples James and John saw this they asked, "Lord, do you want us to call down fire from heaven to consume them?" Jesus turned and rebuked them, and they journeyed to another village.

As they were proceeding on their journey someone said to him, "I will follow you wherever you go." Jesus answered him, "Foxes have dens and birds of the sky have nests, but the Son of Man has nowhere to rest his head."

And to another he said, "Follow me." But he replied, "Lord, let me go first and bury my father." But he answered him, "Let the dead bury their dead. But you, go and proclaim the kingdom of God." And another said, "I will follow you, Lord, but first let me say farewell to my family at home." To him Jesus said, "No one who sets a hand to the plow and looks to what was left behind is fit for the kingdom of God."

First Reading (1 Kgs 19:16b, 19-21)

The LORD said to Elijah: "You shall anoint Elisha, son of Shaphat of Abel-meholah, as prophet to succeed you."

Elijah set out and came upon Elisha, son of Shaphat, as he was plowing with twelve yoke of oxen; he was following the twelfth. Elijah went over to him and threw his cloak over him. Elisha left the oxen, ran after Elijah, and said, "Please, let me kiss my father and mother goodbye, and I will follow you." Elijah answered, "Go back! Have I done anything to you?" Elisha left him and, taking the yoke of oxen, slaughtered them; he used the plowing equipment for fuel to boil their flesh, and gave it to his people to eat. Then Elisha left and followed Elijah as his attendant.

Responsorial Psalm (Ps 16:1-2, 5, 7-8, 9-10, 11)

R̸. (cf. 5a) You are my inheritance, O Lord.

Keep me, O God, for in you I take refuge;
   I say to the LORD, "My Lord are you.

O L<small>ORD</small>, my allotted portion and my cup,
 you it is who hold fast my lot."

R︎. You are my inheritance, O Lord.

I bless the L<small>ORD</small> who counsels me;
 even in the night my heart exhorts me.
I set the L<small>ORD</small> ever before me;
 with him at my right hand I shall not be disturbed.

R︎. You are my inheritance, O Lord.

Therefore my heart is glad and my soul rejoices,
 my body, too, abides in confidence
because you will not abandon my soul to the netherworld,
 nor will you suffer your faithful one to undergo corruption.

R︎. You are my inheritance, O Lord.

You will show me the path to life,
 fullness of joys in your presence,
 the delights at your right hand forever.

R︎. You are my inheritance, O Lord.

Second Reading (Gal 5:1, 13-18)

Reflecting on Living the Gospel

Following Jesus requires much more than simply walking with him from village to village. Following Jesus calls for being "resolutely determined" to journey all the way with him to Jerusalem—and beyond. Any excuses, no matter how seemingly legitimate, keep us from letting go of where we are and embracing where we must go. To be on this journey requires total self-surrender to what Jerusalem holds as well as to "being taken up" into what is "beyond" Jerusalem: the new Jerusalem, "the kingdom of God" fulfilled.

Connecting the Responsorial Psalm to the Readings

Confronted with the urgency of God's call, Elisha abandoned everything and followed Elijah without hesitation, leaving no possessions intact, not stopping even to bid his parents good-bye (first reading). Similarly, the gospel reveals how radically pressing the journey to Jerusalem is for Jesus. Jesus waits for nothing and no one, wastes no time on those unable to receive him, and cuts no slack for those who hesitate to follow him. For Jesus the urgency of the kingdom overrides everything else.

The responsorial psalm reveals what it is that enables Jesus and Elisha to so radically abandon all for the sake of the kingdom. They can relinquish everything, even what seems necessary for a safe and happy life (home and homeland, family and possessions), because they know they possess the very person of God (psalm refrain). They abandon all because they have been given even more. In this gospel Jesus asks us to make the same choice. Full of divine promise and presence, the psalm gives us the courage to say yes. May it become our journey-to-Jerusalem song.

Psalmist Preparation

Your singing of this psalm testifies that you have come to know that the reward of discipleship is far more valuable than its cost. Because you have chosen to follow Jesus, you have been given God's very self as your "portion" and "lot." How have you come to know this? Who has shown you? Whom might you show?

Prayer

God of salvation, you are relentless in calling us to participate in the mission of your Son Jesus. Make us relentless in responding and resolute in fidelity until all peoples share with us your promised inheritance. We ask this in his name. Amen.

Gospel (Luke 10:1-12, 17-20 [or Luke 10:1-9]; L102C)

At that time the Lord appointed seventy-two others whom he sent ahead of him in pairs to every town and place he intended to visit. He said to them, "The harvest is abundant but the laborers are few; so ask the master of the harvest to send out laborers for his harvest. Go on your way; behold, I am sending you like lambs among wolves. Carry no money bag, no sack, no sandals; and greet no one along the way. Into whatever house you enter, first say, 'Peace to this household.' If a peaceful person lives there, your peace will rest on him; but if not, it will return to you. Stay in the same house and eat and drink what is offered to you, for the laborer deserves his payment. Do not move about from one house to another. Whatever town you enter and they welcome you, eat what is set before you, cure the sick in it and say to them, 'The kingdom of God is at hand for you.' Whatever town you enter and they do not receive you, go out into the streets and say, 'The dust of your town that clings to our feet, even that we shake off against you.' Yet know this: the kingdom of God is at hand. I tell you, it will be more tolerable for Sodom on that day than for that town."

The seventy-two returned rejoicing, and said, "Lord, even the demons are subject to us because of your name." Jesus said, "I have observed Satan fall like lightning from the sky. Behold, I have given you the power to 'tread upon serpents' and scorpions and upon the full force of the enemy and nothing will harm you. Nevertheless, do not rejoice because the spirits are subject to you, but rejoice because your names are written in heaven."

First Reading (Isa 66:10-14c)

Thus says the LORD:
    Rejoice with Jerusalem and be glad because of her,
        all you who love her;
    exult, exult with her,
        all you who were mourning over her!
    Oh, that you may suck fully
        of the milk of her comfort,

that you may nurse with delight
    at her abundant breasts!
    For thus says the LORD:
Lo, I will spread prosperity over Jerusalem like a river,
    and the wealth of the nations like an overflowing torrent.
As nurslings, you shall be carried in her arms,
    and fondled in her lap;
as a mother comforts her child,
    so will I comfort you;
    in Jerusalem you shall find your comfort.

When you see this, your heart shall rejoice
    and your bodies flourish like the grass;
the LORD's power shall be known to his servants.

Responsorial Psalm (Ps 66:1-3, 4-5, 6-7, 16, 20)

R̷. (1) Let all the earth cry out to God with joy.

Shout joyfully to God, all the earth,
    sing praise to the glory of his name;
    proclaim his glorious praise.
Say to God, "How tremendous are your deeds!"

R̷. Let all the earth cry out to God with joy.

"Let all on earth worship and sing praise to you,
    sing praise to your name!"
Come and see the works of God,
    his tremendous deeds among the children of Adam.

R̷. Let all the earth cry out to God with joy.

He has changed the sea into dry land;
    through the river they passed on foot.
Therefore let us rejoice in him.
    He rules by his might forever.

R̷. Let all the earth cry out to God with joy.

Hear now, all you who fear God,
    while I declare what he has done for me.
Blessed be God who refused me not
    my prayer or his kindness!

R̷. Let all the earth cry out to God with joy.

Second Reading (Gal 6:14-18)

Reflecting on Living the Gospel
When Jesus sends disciples forth as "laborers for his harvest," he predicts two responses to their presence. Either disciples will be welcomed and able to minister fruitfully, or they will be rejected and their ministry becomes judgment against the unwelcoming town. In either case, however, the "kingdom of God is at hand." How so? Whether accepted or rejected, disciples "harvest" the "kingdom of God" by their very presence, by their very proclamation of Jesus' name, by their very fidelity to Jesus' mission.

Connecting the Responsorial Psalm to the Readings
In these verses from Psalm 66 the psalmist calls the entire earth to come and see the marvelous works of the Lord and to shout praises for God who has wrought such "tremendous . . . deeds!" In the first reading it is the Lord who calls the people to rejoice over marvelous deeds done on behalf of Jerusalem. In her arms the people will be fed and comforted and will discover how God has acted to save and restore. In the gospel Jesus sends his disciples out to proclaim the same message: God is acting to save, the kingdom is at hand. Some will welcome this message, others will reject it. But regardless of the response, the kingdom of God will not be thwarted: evil will be destroyed, healing will come, and peace will prevail.

Like the disciples, we, too, face failure as well as success as we go about the mission of announcing the Good News of the kingdom. Nonetheless, we "cry out . . . with joy" (psalm refrain) for we know that the indomitable power of God will make the kingdom prevail, and that our names are already "written there" (gospel).

Psalmist Preparation
In this Sunday's gospel Jesus sends the disciples on mission to announce his coming. Your singing of the responsorial psalm is part of that mission, for it is a hymn of praise telling of God's saving deeds. Where have you experienced these deeds in your own life? in the lives of others? How have you announced them to the world?

Prayer
God of redemption, you labor tirelessly for human salvation. Grant us the strength to labor with you to bring the blessings of your kingdom to fruition for all peoples. We ask this through Christ our Lord. Amen.

Gospel (Luke 10:25-37; L105C)

There was a scholar of the law who stood up to test Jesus and said, "Teacher, what must I do to inherit eternal life?" Jesus said to him, "What is written in the law? How do you read it?" He said in reply, "*You shall love the Lord, your God, with all your heart, with all your being, with all your strength, and with all your mind, and your neighbor as yourself.*" He replied to him, "You have answered correctly; do this and you will live."

But because he wished to justify himself, he said to Jesus, "And who is my neighbor?" Jesus replied, "A man fell victim to robbers as he went down from Jerusalem to Jericho. They stripped and beat him and went off leaving him half-dead. A priest happened to be going down that road, but when he saw him, he passed by on the opposite side. Likewise a Levite came to the place, and when he saw him, he passed by on the opposite side. But a Samaritan traveler who came upon him was moved with compassion at the sight. He approached the victim, poured oil and wine over his wounds and bandaged them. Then he lifted him up on his own animal, took him to an inn, and cared for him. The next day he took out two silver coins and gave them to the innkeeper with the instruction, 'Take care of him. If you spend more than what I have given you, I shall repay you on my way back.' Which of these three, in your opinion, was neighbor to the robbers' victim?" He answered, "The one who treated him with mercy." Jesus said to him, "Go and do likewise."

First Reading (Deut 30:10-14)

Moses said to the people: "If only you would heed the voice of the LORD, your God, and keep his commandments and statutes that are written in this book of the law, when you return to the LORD, your God, with all your heart and all your soul.

"For this command that I enjoin on you today is not too mysterious and remote for you. It is not up in the sky, that you should say, 'Who will go up in the sky to get it for us and tell us of it, that we may carry it out?' Nor is it across the sea, that you should say, 'Who will cross the sea to get it for us and tell us of it, that we may carry it out?' No, it is something very near to you, already in your mouths and in your hearts; you have only to carry it out."

Responsorial Psalm
(Ps 69:14, 17, 30-31, 33-34, 36, 37 [or Ps 19:8, 9, 10, 11])

℟. (cf. 33) Turn to the Lord in your need, and you will live.

I pray to you, O LORD,
    for the time of your favor, O God!
In your great kindness answer me
    with your constant help.
Answer me, O LORD, for bounteous is your kindness:
    in your great mercy turn toward me.

℟. Turn to the Lord in your need, and you will live.

I am afflicted and in pain;
    let your saving help, O God, protect me.
I will praise the name of God in song,
    and I will glorify him with thanksgiving.

℟. Turn to the Lord in your need, and you will live.

"See, you lowly ones, and be glad;
    you who seek God, may your hearts revive!
For the LORD hears the poor,
    and his own who are in bonds he spurns not."

℟. Turn to the Lord in your need, and you will live.

For God will save Zion
    and rebuild the cities of Judah.
The descendants of his servants shall inherit it,
    and those who love his name shall inhabit it.

℟. Turn to the Lord in your need, and you will live.

Second Reading (Col 1:15-20)

Reflecting on Living the Gospel
The generosity of the Good Samaritan goes way beyond expected neighborliness and simple human compassion. He personally cares for the victim: tending to his wounds, carrying him on his own animal, caring for him at the inn. Yet even this is not enough: he leaves money for his continued care. By this parable Jesus teaches that to inherit "eternal life" we must go beyond who we love and how we love them. We must love as God loves: personally, extravagantly, continually.

Connecting the Responsorial Psalm to the Readings

At first glance Psalm 69 (the first of two choices given in the Lectionary for this Sunday) seems unrelated to either the first reading or the gospel, but deeper reflection reveals the connection. In the first reading Moses counsels the people that the commandments are not beyond them, but within them. In the gospel Jesus teaches that the commandments to love God and neighbor are not hazy, but clear and applicable: to love God means to love the immediate neighbor in need. The verses from Psalm 69 remind us that whenever we have been in need God has responded un-hesitatingly. We know God's law of love because we have experienced God loving us, directly and personally. And we know who is the neighbor in need because we have been that neighbor. It is this knowledge that fills our hearts and inspires us to act compassionately toward others. Psalm 69 grounds our loving in the One who has first, and always, loved us.

Psalmist Preparation

To love one's neighbor as oneself is a tall order, and even more so when that neighbor is a stranger or an enemy. But you have only to turn to God for the strength you need to love in this way (see psalm refrain). When has the grace of God helped you love a neighbor in need?

Prayer

God of compassion, you have planted your law of love in our hearts. Lead us to enflesh this law in acts of compassion to those in need, whether far or near, stranger or friend. We ask this through Christ our Lord. Amen.

Gospel (Luke 10:38-42; L108C)

Jesus entered a village where a woman whose name was
Martha welcomed him. She had a sister named
Mary who sat beside the Lord at his feet listening to
him speak. Martha, burdened with much serving,
came to him and said, "Lord, do you not care that
my sister has left me by myself to do the serving?
Tell her to help me." The Lord said to her in reply,
"Martha, Martha, you are anxious and worried
about many things. There is need of only one
thing. Mary has chosen the better part and it
will not be taken from her."

First Reading (Gen 18:1-10a)

The LORD appeared to Abraham by the terebinth of Mamre, as he sat in
the entrance of his tent, while the day was growing hot. Looking up,
Abraham saw three men standing nearby. When he saw them, he ran
from the entrance of the tent to greet them; and bowing to the ground,
he said: "Sir, if I may ask you this favor, please do not go on past your
servant. Let some water be brought, that you may bathe your feet, and
then rest yourselves under the tree. Now that you have come this close to
your servant, let me bring you a little food, that you may refresh yourselves; and afterward you may go on your way." The men replied,
"Very well, do as you have said."

Abraham hastened into the tent and told Sarah, "Quick, three measures
of fine flour! Knead it and make rolls." He ran to the herd, picked out a
tender, choice steer, and gave it to a servant, who quickly prepared it.
Then Abraham got some curds and milk, as well as the steer that had
been prepared, and set these before the three men; and he waited on
them under the tree while they ate.

They asked Abraham, "Where is your wife Sarah?" He replied, "There
in the tent." One of them said, "I will surely return to you about this time
next year, and Sarah will then have a son."

Responsorial Psalm (Ps 15:2-3, 3-4, 5)

R̠. (1a) He who does justice will live in the presence of the Lord.

One who walks blamelessly and does justice;
> who thinks the truth in his heart
> and slanders not with his tongue.

R̠. He who does justice will live in the presence of the Lord.

Who harms not his fellow man,
> nor takes up a reproach against his neighbor;
by whom the reprobate is despised,
> while he honors those who fear the LORD.

R̠. He who does justice will live in the presence of the Lord.

Who lends not his money at usury
> and accepts no bribe against the innocent.
One who does these things
> shall never be disturbed.

R̠. He who does justice will live in the presence of the Lord.

Second Reading (Col 1:24-28)

Reflecting on Living the Gospel

Jesus tells Martha in this gospel that there "is need of only one thing."
What is it? On the surface, the answer would seem to be "listening to
him speak," as Mary is doing. However, we must also heed how Jesus
judges Martha: "you are anxious and worried about many things." The
"one thing" is to be single-minded, single-hearted, open-minded, open-
hearted. The "one thing" is to surrender ourselves to Jesus' Presence,
whether sitting or standing, resting or working, receiving or giving.

Connecting the Responsorial Psalm to the Readings

Psalm 15 was part of a ritual followed when a person wished to gain ad-
mittance to the temple. Because the temple was God's dwelling, no one
could enter without permission. The individual was questioned at the
gate by a priest who would ask, "LORD, who may abide in your tent?" (v. 1
of Psalm 15, omitted in the Lectionary). The person then answered by re-
citing subsequent verses of the psalm: one who does justice, thinks
truth, slanders not, and so forth. This ritual expressed Israel's understanding that entrance into God's dwelling place required right living.

In the first reading Abraham stands as a type of the right living which grants entrance into the divine presence. He receives strangers with hospitality and is blessed for it. That he responds so immediately to their needs, however, indicates he was already living "in the presence of the Lord" (psalm refrain). Such was the consistent orientation of his life. This is the orientation to which the psalm calls us and to which Jesus calls us when he praises Mary's choice of the "better part" in the gospel. May our abiding desire be to live in the presence of God and may that Presence shape our manner of living.

Psalmist Preparation

In preparing to sing this responsorial psalm, spend some time reflecting on how you choose to live in the presence of God and how that choice shapes your manner of living. When and how do you take time to be with God? How, in concrete ways, do you let God's presence challenge your living?

Prayer

Loving God, you are ever present in our homes and in our hearts. May your presence guide our manner of living so that our homes always be hospitable and our hearts always be attentive to your word. We ask this through Christ our Lord. Amen.

Gospel (Luke 11:1-13; L111C)

Jesus was praying in a certain place, and when he had finished, one of his disciples said to him, "Lord, teach us to pray just as John taught his disciples." He said to them, "When you pray, say:

Father, hallowed be your name,
　　your kingdom come.
　Give us each day our daily
　　　bread
　and forgive us our sins
　for we ourselves forgive everyone in
　　　debt to us,
　and do not subject us to the final test."

And he said to them, "Suppose one of you has a friend to whom he goes at midnight and says, 'Friend, lend me three loaves of bread, for a friend of mine has arrived at my house from a journey and I have nothing to offer him,' and he says in reply from within, 'Do not bother me; the door has already been locked and my children and I are already in bed. I cannot get up to give you anything.' I tell you, if he does not get up to give the visitor the loaves because of their friendship, he will get up to give him whatever he needs because of his persistence.

"And I tell you, ask and you will receive; seek and you will find; knock and the door will be opened to you. For everyone who asks, receives; and the one who seeks, finds; and to the one who knocks, the door will be opened. What father among you would hand his son a snake when he asks for a fish? Or hand him a scorpion when he asks for an egg? If you then, who are wicked, know how to give good gifts to your children, how much more will the Father in heaven give the Holy Spirit to those who ask him?"

First Reading (Gen 18:20-32)

In those days, the LORD said: "The outcry against Sodom and Gomorrah is so great, and their sin so grave, that I must go down and see whether or not their actions fully correspond to the cry against them that comes to me. I mean to find out."

While Abraham's visitors walked on farther toward Sodom, the LORD remained standing before Abraham. Then Abraham drew nearer and said: "Will you sweep away the innocent with the guilty? Suppose there were fifty innocent people in the city; would you wipe out the place, rather than spare it for the sake of the fifty innocent people within it? Far be it from you to do such a thing, to make the innocent die with the guilty so that the innocent and the guilty would be treated alike! Should not the judge of all the world act with justice?" The LORD replied, "If I find fifty innocent people in the city of Sodom, I will spare the whole place for their sake." Abraham spoke up again: "See how I am presuming to speak to my Lord, though I am but dust and ashes! What if there are five less than fifty innocent people? Will you destroy the whole city because of those five?" He answered, "I will not destroy it, if I find forty-five there." But Abraham persisted, saying, "What if only forty are found there?" He replied, "I will forbear doing it for the sake of the forty." Then Abraham said, "Let not my Lord grow impatient if I go on. What if only thirty are found there?" He replied, "I will forbear doing it if I can find but thirty there." Still Abraham went on, "Since I have thus dared to speak to my Lord, what if there are no more than twenty?" The LORD answered, "I will not destroy it, for the sake of the twenty." But he still persisted: "Please, let not my Lord grow angry if I speak up this last time. What if there are at least ten there?" He replied, "For the sake of those ten, I will not destroy it."

Responsorial Psalm (Ps 138:1-2, 2-3, 6-7, 7-8)

R̶. (3a) Lord, on the day I called for help, you answered me.

I will give thanks to you, O LORD, with all my heart,
   for you have heard the words of my mouth;
   in the presence of the angels I will sing your praise;
I will worship at your holy temple
   and give thanks to your name.

R̶. Lord, on the day I called for help, you answered me.

Because of your kindness and your truth;
   for you have made great above all things
   your name and your promise.
When I called you answered me;
   you built up strength within me.

R̶. Lord, on the day I called for help, you answered me.

The LORD is exalted, yet the lowly he sees,
   and the proud he knows from afar.
Though I walk amid distress, you preserve me;
   against the anger of my enemies you raise your hand.

R̶. Lord, on the day I called for help, you answered me.

Your right hand saves me.

The LORD will complete what he has done for me;
your kindness, O LORD, endures forever;

forsake not the work of your hands.

R7. Lord, on the day I called for help, you answered me.

Second Reading (Col 2:12-14)

Reflecting on Living the Gospel

Jesus' disciples want him to teach them to pray "just as John taught his disciples." Jesus couldn't teach them the prayer of John, however, because he was not John. Jesus' prayer to his Father flows from who he is—the One who praises, intercedes, forgives, reconciles, and protects. In the end, his prayer is for his Father to "give the Holy Spirit." Then, no request is too great, no seeking is unrewarded, no door is locked.

Connecting the Responsorial Psalm to the Readings

In the gospel Jesus responds on several levels to the disciples' request that he show them how to pray: he teaches them the Our Father; he encourages them to be persistent; he subtly suggests what it is they are to pray for (the gift of the Holy Spirit); and he calls them to ground their prayer in the goodness of God who is their Father. The first reading gives us a dramatic example of such prayer. Abraham persists in his petition. He remains humble yet audacious, speaking to God directly and forcefully. Finally, what he prays for is righteous judgment and protection of the innocent. On the divine side the story reveals that God waits for such prayer. God stands directly in front of Abraham and invites the conversation. God listens each time Abraham speaks and grants his request. Clearly this is a God who desires salvation and who seeks human collaboration in bringing it about.

The responsorial psalm confirms that what grounds confidence in prayer is the nature of God who is great in kindness and true to every promise. God will answer when we call; God will complete the work of salvation begun in us. We need have no hesitation to petition such a God. We need only to carefully discern for what it is we ask.

Psalmist Preparation

When you sing the responsorial psalm, what the assembly hears more than the beauty of your voice is the sound of your praying. Ask Christ this week to teach you how to pray the psalm.

Prayer

God who answers all prayer, keep us persistent in our petitions and audacious in addressing them to you. Above all, teach us for what we are to pray so that your will may be done and your kingdom may come. We ask this through Christ our Lord. Amen.

Gospel (Luke 12:13-21; L114C)

Someone in the crowd said to Jesus, "Teacher, tell my brother to share the inheritance with me." He replied to him, "Friend, who appointed me as your judge and arbitrator?" Then he said to the crowd, "Take care to guard against all greed, for though one may be rich, one's life does not consist of possessions."

Then he told them a parable. "There was a rich man whose land produced a bountiful harvest. He asked himself, 'What shall I do, for I do not have space to store my harvest?' And he said, 'This is what I shall do: I shall tear down my barns and build larger ones. There I shall store all my grain and other goods and I shall say to myself, "Now as for you, you have so many good things stored up for many years, rest, eat, drink, be merry!"' But God said to him, 'You fool, this night your life will be demanded of you; and the things you have prepared, to whom will they belong?' Thus will it be for all who store up treasure for themselves but are not rich in what matters to God."

First Reading (Eccl 1:2; 2:21-23)

Vanity of vanities, says Qoheleth,
   vanity of vanities! All things are vanity!

Here is one who has labored with wisdom and knowledge and skill, and yet to another who has not labored over it, he must leave property. This also is vanity and a great misfortune. For what profit comes to man from all the toil and anxiety of heart with which he has labored under the sun? All his days sorrow and grief are his occupation; even at night his mind is not at rest. This also is vanity.

Responsorial Psalm (Ps 90:3-4, 5-6, 12-13, 14 and 17)

R̶. (8) If today you hear his voice, harden not your hearts.

You turn man back to dust,
   saying, "Return, O children of men."
For a thousand years in your sight
   are as yesterday, now that it is past,
   or as a watch of the night.

R̶. If today you hear his voice, harden not your hearts.

You make an end of them in their sleep;
    the next morning they are like the changing grass,
which at dawn springs up anew,
    but by evening wilts and fades.

R℣. If today you hear his voice, harden not your hearts.

Teach us to number our days aright,
    that we may gain wisdom of heart.
Return, O LORD! How long?
    Have pity on your servants!

R℣. If today you hear his voice, harden not your hearts.

Fill us at daybreak with your kindness,
    that we may shout for joy and gladness all our days.
And may the gracious care of the LORD our God be ours;
    prosper the work of our hands for us!
    Prosper the work of our hands!

R℣. If today you hear his voice, harden not your hearts.

Second Reading (Col 3:1-5, 9-11)

Reflecting on Living the Gospel
The rich man in the gospel thinks building bigger barns to hold a boon
of "grain and other goods" will give him enough security that he can
"rest, eat, drink, be merry." He is misguided about the bigger barn he
really needs to build. In the end, what "matters to God" is a "barn" full
of what only God can give: life, love, holiness, fidelity, generosity, compassion, Life. No barn can ever be big enough to hold these.

Connecting the Responsorial Psalm to the Readings
Psalm 90, from which this responsorial psalm is taken, contrasts the sta-
bility and steadfastness of God with the uncertainty and transience of
human life. The verses used in the Lectionary express Israel's prayer that
God teach them true assessment of their life and work. As the reading
from Ecclesiastes indicates, they already realize hard work and physical
possessions give no sure value. What is worth possessing is the kind and
"gracious care" of God (psalm). Jesus affirms this stance when he challenges his hearers to turn from evaluating their worth based on physical
possessions to evaluating it based on being "rich in what matters to
God" (gospel).

It is significant that the psalm refrain is taken not from Psalm 90 but from Psalm 95, a psalm which refers to the infidelity of Israel's ancestors during their desert exodus from slavery to the Promised Land. No matter how much God gave them (water, manna), they constantly whined that they did not have enough. The Lectionary's choice of this refrain is acknowledgment that reckoning our days and assessing our worth in God's terms is a challenging task. May this be the work God prospers in us (psalm).

Psalmist Preparation

The refrain for this responsorial psalm is particularly challenging. Sometimes when you hear God's voice, your heart hardens. When do you experience this happening for yourself? How does God help you hear in spite of your resistance?

Prayer

Loving God, you offer us abundant life in you. Teach us to treasure you above all other possessions and to work for the fulfillment of your will on earth. We ask this through Christ our Lord. Amen.

NINETEENTH SUNDAY IN ORDINARY TIME

AUGUST 7, 2016

Gospel (Luke 12:32-48 [or Luke 12:35-40]; L117C)

Jesus said to his disciples: "Do not be afraid any longer, little flock, for your Father is pleased to give you the kingdom. Sell your belongings and give alms. Provide money bags for yourselves that do not wear out, an inexhaustible treasure in heaven that no thief can reach nor moth destroy. For where your treasure is, there also will your heart be.

"Gird your loins and light your lamps and be like servants who await their master's return from a wedding, ready to open immediately when he comes and knocks. Blessed are those servants whom the master finds vigilant on his arrival. Amen, I say to you, he will gird himself, have them recline at table, and proceed to wait on them. And should he come in the second or third watch and find them prepared in this way, blessed are those servants. Be sure of this: if the master of the house had known the hour when the thief was coming, he would not have let his house be broken into. You also must be prepared, for at an hour you do not expect, the Son of Man will come."

Then Peter said, "Lord, is this parable meant for us or for everyone?" And the Lord replied, "Who, then, is the faithful and prudent steward whom the master will put in charge of his servants to distribute the food allowance at the proper time? Blessed is that servant whom his master on arrival finds doing so. Truly, I say to you, the master will put the servant in charge of all his property. But if that servant says to himself, 'My master is delayed in coming,' and begins to beat the menservants and the maidservants, to eat and drink and get drunk, then that servant's master will come on an unexpected day and at an unknown hour and will punish the servant severely and assign him a place with the unfaithful. That servant who knew his master's will but did not make preparations nor act in accord with his will shall be beaten severely; and the servant who was ignorant of his master's will but acted in a way deserving of a severe beating shall be beaten only lightly. Much will be required of the person entrusted with much, and still more will be demanded of the person entrusted with more."

153

First Reading (Wis 18:6-9)

The night of the passover was known beforehand to our fathers,
  that, with sure knowledge of the oaths in which they put their faith,
  they might have courage.
Your people awaited the salvation of the just
  and the destruction of their foes.
For when you punished our adversaries,
  in this you glorified us whom you had summoned.
For in secret the holy children of the good were offering sacrifice
  and putting into effect with one accord the divine institution.

Responsorial Psalm (Ps 33:1, 12, 18-19, 20-22)

R̸. (12b) Blessed the people the Lord has chosen to be his own.

Exult, you just, in the LORD;
  praise from the upright is fitting.
Blessed the nation whose God is the LORD,
  the people he has chosen for his own inheritance.

R̸. Blessed the people the Lord has chosen to be his own.

See, the eyes of the LORD are upon those who fear him,
  upon those who hope for his kindness,
to deliver them from death
  and preserve them in spite of famine.

R̸. Blessed the people the Lord has chosen to be his own.

Our soul waits for the LORD,
  who is our help and our shield.
May your kindness, O LORD, be upon us
  who have put our hope in you.

R̸. Blessed the people the Lord has chosen to be his own.

Second Reading (Heb 11:1-2, 8-19 [or Heb 11:1-2, 8-12])

Reflecting on Living the Gospel

In both of these parables about a master's absence, the critical issue is what the servants do while the master is away. They must be vigilant for the "master's return" and faithful in doing "the master's will." Even when the master is absent, servants who have appropriated his way of life will act as if the master were present. To belong to Jesus' household—God's kingdom—we must appropriate Jesus' way of life. We are to be his living, saving Presence. In us, he is never absent.

Connecting the Responsorial Psalm to the Readings

Jesus tells us in this Sunday's gospel that where our treasure is there our heart will be. Along this very line the responsorial psalm says something remarkable about God: we are God's treasure, chosen as "his own inheritance." And where God's treasure is, God's heart will be.

This is the reason why we can wait with hope and "sure knowledge" for the deliverance promised us, whether we know the hour of its arrival (first reading) or not (gospel). God has chosen us and already given us the kingdom (gospel). Our response is to keep our eyes turned toward the God whose eyes are fixed upon us (psalm), remaining faithful servants who fulfill the Lord's will in season and out (gospel).

Psalmist Preparation

Preparing to sing the responsorial psalm means more than learning new words and music. Far more, it means preparing yourself for the coming of Christ in the Liturgy of the Word. No matter how many times you have sung a particular psalm, no matter how many times you have heard the proclamation of a particular gospel, there is always a new coming of Christ. May you be a vigilant and faithful servant!

Prayer

God, our inheritance, you keep your eyes fixed on us. Keep our eyes fixed on you so that Christ may find us faithful and ready on the day of his return. We ask this in his name. Amen.

Gospel (Luke 12:49-53; L120C)

Jesus said to his disciples: "I have come to set the earth on fire, and how I wish it were already blazing! There is a baptism with which I must be baptized, and how great is my anguish until it is accomplished! Do you think that I have come to establish peace on the earth? No, I tell you, but rather division. From now on a household of five will be divided, three against two and two against three; a father will be divided against his son and a son against his father, a mother against her daughter and a daughter against her mother, a mother-in-law against her daughter-in-law and a daughter-in-law against her mother-in-law."

First Reading (Jer 38:4-6, 8-10)

In those days, the princes said to the king: "Jeremiah ought to be put to death; he is demoralizing the soldiers who are left in this city, and all the people, by speaking such things to them; he is not interested in the welfare of our people, but in their ruin." King Zedekiah answered: "He is in your power"; for the king could do nothing with them. And so they took Jeremiah and threw him into the cistern of Prince Malchiah, which was in the quarters of the guard, letting him down with ropes. There was no water in the cistern, only mud, and Jeremiah sank into the mud.

Ebed-melech, a court official, went there from the palace and said to him: "My lord king, these men have been at fault in all they have done to the prophet Jeremiah, casting him into the cistern. He will die of famine on the spot, for there is no more food in the city." Then the king ordered Ebed-melech the Cushite to take three men along with him, and draw the prophet Jeremiah out of the cistern before he should die.

Responsorial Psalm (Ps 40:2, 3, 4, 18)

R℣. (14b) Lord, come to my aid!

I have waited, waited for the LORD,
    and he stooped toward me.

R℣. Lord, come to my aid!

The LORD heard my cry.
He drew me out of the pit of destruction,
    out of the mud of the swamp;

he set my feet upon a crag;
  he made firm my steps.

R̸. Lord, come to my aid!

And he put a new song into my mouth,
  a hymn to our God.
Many shall look on in awe
  and trust in the LORD.

R̸. Lord, come to my aid!

Though I am afflicted and poor,
  yet the LORD thinks of me.
You are my help and my deliverer;
  O my God, hold not back!

R̸. Lord, come to my aid!

Second Reading (Heb 12:1-4)

Reflecting on Living the Gospel

This is a bad news, good news gospel. The bad news is that Jesus' coming throws the world headlong into fire, anguish, division. The good news is that, in spite of Jesus speaking to the contrary, he does grant peace—to his disciples after his resurrection. His gift of peace, however, does not eliminate the fire, anguish, and division. These painful consequences of faithful living sharpen the choice each of us must make: to be "baptized" with Jesus into his death—and risen Life.

Connecting the Responsorial Psalm to the Readings

In the first reading Jeremiah is thrown into a muddy cistern because he challenged the leaders of Israel. Jesus tells us in the gospel that we, too, will face extreme opposition if we follow him. Discipleship demands a willingness to stand alone, to be cut off even from those close to us when the call of Christ requires it. But the responsorial psalm reminds us that we are not, in fact, left alone. When human persons turn away from or against us because of our fidelity to discipleship, God will stoop close. Nothing can eradicate the cost of discipleship, but neither can anything destroy God's care for and protection of us. Though we may die, as did Jesus, God will not abandon us to death but will raise us to new life. This psalm expresses our absolute trust that God will "hold . . . back" nothing in our support.

Psalmist Preparation

In this psalm you call upon God to "come to my aid." In the context of the readings, this is a cry raised in face of persecution experienced because you are being faithful to discipleship. When have you found yourself meeting such opposition? What helped you remain faithful? How did God come to your aid?

Prayer

Redeeming God, keep our hearts burning like Christ's for the coming of the kingdom. And when our fidelity to discipleship leads to discord rather than to peace, come to our aid with your care, your protection, and your promise of fullness of life. We ask this through Christ our Lord. Amen.

AUGUST 15, 2016

Gospel (Luke 1:39-56; L622)

Mary set out and traveled to the hill country in haste to a town of Judah, where she entered the house of Zechariah and greeted Elizabeth. When Elizabeth heard Mary's greeting, the infant leaped in her womb, and Elizabeth, filled with the Holy Spirit, cried out in a loud voice and said, "Blessed are you among women, and blessed is the fruit of your womb. And how does this happen to me, that the mother of my Lord should come to me? For at the moment the sound of your greeting reached my ears, the infant in my womb leaped for joy. Blessed are you who believed that what was spoken to you by the Lord would be fulfilled."

And Mary said:

"My soul proclaims the greatness of the Lord;
my spirit rejoices in God my Savior
for he has looked with favor on his lowly servant.
From this day all generations will call me blessed:
the Almighty has done great things for me,
and holy is his Name.
He has mercy on those who fear him
in every generation.
He has shown the strength of his arm,
and has scattered the proud in their conceit.
He has cast down the mighty from their thrones,
and has lifted up the lowly.
He has filled the hungry with good things,
and the rich he has sent away empty.
He has come to the help of his servant Israel
for he has remembered his promise of mercy,
the promise he made to our fathers,
to Abraham and his children forever."

Mary remained with her about three months and then returned to her home.

First Reading (Rev 11:19a; 12:1-6a, 10ab)

God's temple in heaven was opened, and the ark of his covenant could be seen in the temple.

A great sign appeared in the sky, a woman clothed with the sun, with the moon under her feet, and on her head a crown of twelve stars. She was with child and wailed aloud in pain as she labored to give birth. Then another sign appeared in the sky; it was a huge red dragon, with seven heads and ten horns, and on its heads were seven diadems. Its tail swept away a third of the stars in the sky and hurled them down to the earth. Then the dragon stood before the woman about to give birth, to devour her child when she gave birth. She gave birth to a son, a male child, destined to rule all the nations with an iron rod. Her child was caught up to God and his throne. The woman herself fled into the desert where she had a place prepared by God.

Then I heard a loud voice in heaven say:

"Now have salvation and power come,
  and the Kingdom of our God
  and the authority of his Anointed One."

Responsorial Psalm (Ps 45:10, 11, 12, 16)

℞. (10bc) The queen stands at your right hand, arrayed in gold.

The queen takes her place at your right hand in gold of Ophir.

℞. The queen stands at your right hand, arrayed in gold.

Hear, O daughter, and see; turn your ear,
  forget your people and your father's house.

℞. The queen stands at your right hand, arrayed in gold.

So shall the king desire your beauty;
  for he is your lord.

℞. The queen stands at your right hand, arrayed in gold.

They are borne in with gladness and joy;
  they enter the palace of the king.

℞. The queen stands at your right hand, arrayed in gold.

See Appendix, p. 217, for Second Reading

Reflecting on Living the Gospel

What a greeting Mary gave Elizabeth that the infant in her womb "leaped for joy"! This could not have been any ordinary greeting. Hers was a greeting begotten by belief, by yes, by encounter. Hers was a greeting that proclaimed God's mighty deeds then and now. Hers was a greeting that announced the Presence of the dawning of salvation. Hers is a greeting still spoken and being fulfilled today. Hers is a greeting we must hear. Do we hear the greeting? Are we leaping for joy?

Connecting the Responsorial Psalm to the Readings

Psalm 45 was a nuptial psalm used in the wedding ceremony between an Israelite king and his bride. The people called upon the bride to forget her family and homeland and embrace a new and more glorious relationship. She chose to do so, but not alone: with "gladness and joy" an entire retinue followed her.

By accepting her role in the incarnation, Mary chose to engage in the cosmic struggle between the forces of evil and the saving power of God (first reading). Blessed is she for believing in the power and promise of God even when these seemed hidden from view (gospel). Blessed is she for not clinging to past and present and venturing in hope into an unseen future. Now the victory of Christ over sin and death is completed in her (second reading) and God celebrates her beauty (psalm). In her, the lowly have been lifted up and the hungering satisfied (gospel). In her, humanity has been wedded to God. And we belong to the retinue.

Psalmist Preparation

As you sing this responsorial psalm, you celebrate your own entrance into heaven, for the entire church is borne with Mary into God's kingdom. How can you prepare yourself to sing such promise and glory? How can you imitate Mary more fully in her choice to cooperate with God's plan for salvation?

Prayer

Glorious God, the victory of your Son over sin and death has been completed in Mary, whom you raised to your right hand in heaven. May we, like her, always say *yes* to your holy will that one day we may share in her glory. We ask this through Christ our Lord. Amen.

Gospel (Luke 13:22-30; L123C)

Jesus passed through towns and villages, teaching as he went and making his way to Jerusalem. Someone asked him, "Lord, will only a few people be saved?" He answered them, "Strive to enter through the narrow gate, for many, I tell you, will attempt to enter but will not be strong enough. After the master of the house has arisen and locked the door, then will you stand outside knocking and saying, 'Lord, open the door for us.' He will say to you in reply, 'I do not know where you are from.' And you will say, 'We ate and drank in your company and you taught in our streets.' Then he will say to you, 'I do not know where you are from. Depart from me, all you evildoers!' And there will be wailing and grinding of teeth when you see Abraham, Isaac, and Jacob and all the prophets in the kingdom of God and you yourselves cast out. And people will come from the east and the west and from the north and the south and will recline at table in the kingdom of God. For behold, some are last who will be first, and some are first who will be last."

First Reading (Isa 66:18-21)

Thus says the LORD: I know their works and their thoughts, and I come to gather nations of every language; they shall come and see my glory. I will set a sign among them; from them I will send fugitives to the nations: to Tarshish, Put and Lud, Mosoch, Tubal and Javan, to the distant coastlands that have never heard of my fame, or seen my glory; and they shall proclaim my glory among the nations. They shall bring all your brothers and sisters from all the nations as an offering to the LORD, on horses and in chariots, in carts, upon mules and dromedaries, to Jerusalem, my holy mountain, says the LORD, just as the Israelites bring their offering to the house of the LORD in clean vessels. Some of these I will take as priests and Levites, says the LORD.

Responsorial Psalm (Ps 117:1, 2)

R℣. (Mark 16:15) Go out to all the world and tell the Good News.
or: R℣. Alleluia.

Praise the LORD, all you nations;
     glorify him, all you peoples!

R̸. Go out to all the world and tell the Good News. *or:* R̸. Alleluia.

For steadfast is his kindness toward us,
     and the fidelity of the LORD endures forever.

R̸. Go out to all the world and tell the Good News. *or:* R̸. Alleluia.

Second Reading (Heb 12:5-7, 11-13)

Reflecting on Living the Gospel
What strength is needed to enter "through the narrow gate," the locked door? The strength that comes from living so that the "master of the house" knows us and opens to us. The strength that comes from faithfully living "in the kingdom of God." This strength only comes from God, who offers it to everyone. Because of this strength we choose to journey "to Jerusalem"; we choose to pass through death to Life.

Connecting the Responsorial Psalm to the Readings
Jesus challenges us in this Sunday's gospel with the harsh reality that not everyone will be admitted to the kingdom of God (gospel). His message, however, is for those who have heard the Good News of salvation, not for those who have "never heard of [God's] fame, or seen [God's] glory" (first reading). To these God will send messengers to tell them the Good News and gather them to the holy dwelling, Jerusalem. For those who have already heard, radical demands are in place (Jesus has been spelling these out in previous Sundays' gospels). And the responsorial psalm gives yet another command: we are to be the messengers who spread the Good News of God's salvation to all the world. The psalm reminds us that we are a necessary part of God's plan of salvation for all. It also suggests that we cannot recline at God's table if we have not invited everyone else to be there with us.

Psalmist Preparation
In singing this psalm you command the assembly to tell the world the Good News of salvation. Who in your life is especially in need of hearing this news? How do you tell them?

Prayer
Saving God, you invite all people to your heavenly banquet. Embolden us to preach this Good News to all the world, and fortify us to remain faithful to its demands. We ask this through Christ our Lord. Amen.

Gospel (Luke 14:1, 7-14; L126C)

On a sabbath Jesus went to dine at the home of one of the leading Pharisees, and the people there were observing him carefully.

He told a parable to those who had been invited, noticing how they were choosing the places of honor at the table. "When you are invited by someone to a wedding banquet, do not recline at table in the place of honor. A more distinguished guest than you may have been invited by him, and the host who invited both of you may approach you and say, 'Give your place to this man,' and then you would proceed with embarrassment to take the lowest place. Rather, when you are invited, go and take the lowest place so that when the host comes to you he may say, 'My friend, move up to a higher position.' Then you will enjoy the esteem of your companions at the table. For everyone who exalts himself will be humbled, but the one who humbles himself will be exalted." Then he said to the host who invited him, "When you hold a lunch or a dinner, do not invite your friends or your brothers or your relatives or your wealthy neighbors, in case they may invite you back and you have repayment. Rather, when you hold a banquet, invite the poor, the crippled, the lame, the blind; blessed indeed will you be because of their inability to repay you. For you will be repaid at the resurrection of the righteous."

First Reading (Sir 3:17-18, 20, 28-29)

My child, conduct your affairs with humility,
   and you will be loved more than a giver of gifts.
Humble yourself the more, the greater you are,
   and you will find favor with God.
What is too sublime for you, seek not,
   into things beyond your strength search not.
The mind of a sage appreciates proverbs,
   and an attentive ear is the joy of the wise.
Water quenches a flaming fire,
   and alms atone for sins.

Responsorial Psalm (Ps 68:4-5, 6-7, 10-11)

R℣. (cf. 11b) God, in your goodness, you have made a home for the poor.

The just rejoice and exult before God;
   they are glad and rejoice.
Sing to God, chant praise to his name;
   whose name is the LORD.

R℣. God, in your goodness, you have made a home for the poor.

The father of orphans and the defender of widows
   is God in his holy dwelling.
God gives a home to the forsaken;
   he leads forth prisoners to prosperity.

R℣. God, in your goodness, you have made a home for the poor.

A bountiful rain you showered down, O God, upon your inheritance;
   you restored the land when it languished;
your flock settled in it;
   in your goodness, O God, you provided it for the needy.

R℣. God, in your goodness, you have made a home for the poor.

Second Reading (Heb 12:18-19, 22-24a)

Reflecting on Living the Gospel
At Jesus' "wedding banquet" *all* who hear and heed Jesus' admonition to humility, inclusivity, and generosity sit in the *one* "place of honor." This "place of honor" is not a limited space, a single seat, a physical arrangement of host and guests one to another. It is a spacious relationship to the risen Jesus that is a share in his divine Life. It is given to "the righteous," all those who have chosen to live and act as Jesus the Host. How blessed are they!

Connecting the Responsorial Psalm to the Readings
In this Sunday's gospel the people were "observing [Jesus] carefully." In the responsorial psalm we observe God carefully. What we see is a God who makes "a home for the poor" and provides "for the needy." When Jesus in the gospel advises us to invite to our table "the poor, the crippled, the lame, the blind," he is challenging us to model what we see God doing. And when we do so we experience a remarkable reversal in our own position. Choosing to give up the first place so that room be made for the poor and needy exalts us. Our humility "find[s] favor with God"

(first reading). Even more, we become like God. When we sing this psalm, then, we are praying to become like the God we praise.

Psalmist Preparation

This psalm praises God for goodness to the poor and needy. Only those who recognize themselves among the poor and needy can see what God is doing to lift them up. How are you poor and needy? How does God lift you up by inviting you to the banquet of Jesus' Body and Blood? How do you invite others to join you at this banquet?

Prayer

Gracious God, you lift up those who are humble. Grant us the humility we need to see ourselves rightly and to look upon the lowly with your care and compassion. We ask this through Christ our Lord. Amen.

Gospel (Luke 14:25-33; L129C)

Great crowds were traveling with Jesus, and he turned and addressed them, "If anyone comes to me without hating his father and mother, wife and children, brothers and sisters, and even his own life, he cannot be my disciple. Whoever does not carry his own cross and come after me cannot be my disciple. Which of you wishing to construct a tower does not first sit down and calculate the cost to see if there is enough for its completion? Otherwise, after laying the foundation and finding himself unable to finish the work the onlookers should laugh at him and say, 'This one began to build but did not have the resources to finish.' Or what king marching into battle would not first sit down and decide whether with ten thousand troops he can successfully oppose another king advancing upon him with twenty thousand troops? But if not, while he is still far away, he will send a delegation to ask for peace terms. In the same way, anyone of you who does not renounce all his possessions cannot be my disciple."

First Reading (Wis 9:13-18b)

Who can know God's counsel,
    or who can conceive what the LORD intends?
For the deliberations of mortals are timid,
    and unsure are our plans.
For the corruptible body burdens the soul
    and the earthen shelter weighs down the mind that has many
        concerns.
And scarce do we guess the things on earth,
    and what is within our grasp we find with difficulty;
    but when things are in heaven, who can search them out?
Or who ever knew your counsel, except you had given wisdom
    and sent your holy spirit from on high?
And thus were the paths of those on earth made straight.

Responsorial Psalm **(Ps 90:3-4, 5-6, 12-13, 14, 17)**

℟. (1) In every age, O Lord, you have been our refuge.

You turn man back to dust,
   saying, "Return, O children of men."
For a thousand years in your sight
   are as yesterday, now that it is past,
   or as a watch of the night.

℟. In every age, O Lord, you have been our refuge.

You make an end of them in their sleep;
   the next morning they are like the changing grass,
which at dawn springs up anew,
   but by evening wilts and fades.

℟. In every age, O Lord, you have been our refuge.

Teach us to number our days aright,
   that we may gain wisdom of heart.
Return, O LORD! How long?
   Have pity on your servants!

℟. In every age, O Lord, you have been our refuge.

Fill us at daybreak with your kindness,
   that we may shout for joy and gladness all our days.
And may the gracious care of the LORD our God be ours;
   prosper the work of our hands for us!
   Prosper the work of our hands!

℟. In every age, O Lord, you have been our refuge.

Second Reading **(Phlm 9-10, 12-17)**

Reflecting on Living the Gospel
Jesus forewarns the "great crowds" traveling with him that they must
"calculate the cost" and the risk of journeying with him to Jerusalem.
Even family relationships cannot come before the demands of following
him. However, we really cannot calculate the cost of discipleship. Yes, we
must follow Jesus with eyes wide open. The cost of discipleship? Everything we have and are. The reward of discipleship? Everything God has
and is.

Connecting the Responsorial Psalm to the Readings

The first reading reminds us of a truth we already know: "the deliberations of mortals are timid, / and unsure." But Jesus challenges us in the
gospel to be neither timid nor unsure when deliberating the cost of discipleship. It is total. Relationships must be abandoned, possessions must
be renounced, the cross must be carried. The responsorial psalm promises, however, that we will not be left with only our own meager strength.
God will grant us "wisdom" and will "prosper the work of our hands."
God will give us both the wisdom to calculate the cost and the courage to
pay it (first reading). God knows the all-encompassing cost of discipleship and will be with us when we need strength, support, encourage-
ment, and mercy. In singing this psalm we profess our confidence in God,
who knows even better than we do what will be exacted of us and who
has promised to see us through.

Psalmist Preparation

The cost of following Christ is radical, but in this psalm you remind the
assembly they have more than themselves to depend upon: their discipleship will prosper because God underwrites it. You sing realistically of
both the tenuousness of human strength and the steadfastness of God.
May your singing give the assembly courage.

Prayer

Steadfast God, our refuge in time of need, when the cost of discipleship
makes our commitment waver, strengthen us; when human weakness
makes us want to avoid the cross, give us courage; when we are tempted
to hold back from you, overwhelm us with your love that we may know
fullness of life. We ask this through Christ our Lord. Amen.

Gospel (Luke 15:1-32 [or Luke 15:1-10]; L132C)

Tax collectors and sinners were all drawing near to listen to Jesus, but the Pharisees and scribes began to complain, saying, "This man welcomes sinners and eats with them." So to them he addressed this parable. "What man among you having a hundred sheep and losing one of them would not leave the ninety-nine in the desert and go after the lost one until he finds it? And when he does find it, he sets it on his shoulders with great joy and, upon his arrival home, he calls together his friends and neighbors and says to them, 'Rejoice with me because I have found my lost sheep.' I tell you, in just the same way there will be more joy in heaven over one sinner who repents than over ninety-nine righteous people who have no need of repentance.

"Or what woman having ten coins and losing one would not light a lamp and sweep the house, searching carefully until she finds it? And when she does find it, she calls together her friends and neighbors and says to them, 'Rejoice with me because I have found the coin that I lost.' In just the same way, I tell you, there will be rejoicing among the angels of God over one sinner who repents."

Then he said, "A man had two sons, and the younger son said to his father, 'Father give me the share of your estate that should come to me.' So the father divided the property between them. After a few days, the younger son collected all his belongings and set off to a distant country where he squandered his inheritance on a life of dissipation. When he had freely spent everything, a severe famine struck that country, and he found himself in dire need. So he hired himself out to one of the local citizens who sent him to his farm to tend the swine. And he longed to eat his fill of the pods on which the swine fed, but nobody gave him any. Coming to his senses he thought, 'How many of my father's hired workers have more than enough food to eat, but here am I, dying from hunger. I shall get up and go to my father and I shall say to him, "Father, I have sinned against heaven and against you. I no longer deserve to be called your son; treat me as you would treat one of your hired workers."' So he got up and went back to his father. While he was still a long way off, his father caught sight of him, and was filled with compassion. He ran to his son, embraced him and kissed him. His son said to him, 'Father, I have sinned against heaven and against you; I no longer deserve to be called your son.' But his father ordered his servants, 'Quickly bring the finest robe and put it on him; put a ring on his finger and sandals on his feet. Take the fattened calf and slaughter it. Then let us celebrate with a feast, because this son of mine was dead, and has come to life again; he was lost, and has been found.' Then the celebration began. Now the older son had been out in the field and, on his way back, as he neared the house, he heard the sound of music and dancing. He called one of the servants and asked what this might mean. The servant said to him, 'Your brother has returned and your father has slaughtered the fattened calf because he has him back safe and sound.' He became angry, and when he refused to enter the house, his father came out and pleaded with him. He said to his father in reply, 'Look, all these years I served you and not once did I disobey your orders; yet you never gave me even a young goat to feast on with my friends. But when your son returns, who swallowed up your property with prostitutes, for him you slaughter the fattened calf.' He said to him, 'My son, you are here with me always; everything I have is yours. But now we must celebrate and rejoice, because your brother was dead and has come to life again; he was lost and has been found.'"

First Reading (Exod 32:7-11, 13-14)

The LORD said to Moses, "Go down at once to your people, whom you brought out of the land of Egypt, for they have become depraved. They have soon turned aside from the way I pointed out to them, making for themselves a molten calf and worshiping it, sacrificing to it and crying out, 'This is your God, O Israel, who brought you out of the land of Egypt!' I see how stiff-necked this people is," continued the LORD to Moses. "Let me alone, then, that my wrath may blaze up against them to consume them. Then I will make of you a great nation."

But Moses implored the LORD, his God, saying, "Why, O LORD, should your wrath blaze up against your own people, whom you brought out of the land of Egypt with such great power and with so strong a hand? Remember your servants Abraham, Isaac, and Israel, and how you swore to them by your own self, saying, 'I will make your descendants as numerous as the stars in the sky; and all this land that I promised, I will give your descendants as their perpetual heritage.'" So the LORD relented in the punishment he had threatened to inflict on his people.

Responsorial Psalm (Ps 51:3-4, 12-13, 17, 19)

R̸. (Luke 15:18) I will rise and go to my father.

Have mercy on me, O God, in your goodness;
    in the greatness of your compassion wipe out my offense.
Thoroughly wash me from my guilt
    and of my sin cleanse me.

R̸. I will rise and go to my father.

A clean heart create for me, O God,
    and a steadfast spirit renew within me.
Cast me not out from your presence,
    and your Holy Spirit take not from me.

R̸. I will rise and go to my father.

O Lord, open my lips,
    and my mouth shall proclaim your praise.
My sacrifice, O God, is a contrite spirit;
    a heart contrite and humbled, O God, you will not spurn.

R̸. I will rise and go to my father.

Second Reading (1 Tim 1:12-17)

Reflecting on Living the Gospel
In this gospel tax collectors and sinners are "drawing near to listen to
Jesus." Pharisees and scribes, on the other hand, observe what is happening and complain to Jesus. He answers their complaint with three parables that turn the table on their belief about who is really saved. Jesus
invites everyone to his table—his feast of mercy. But not everyone
chooses to come. Only those come who recognize their need to be found.

Connecting the Responsorial Psalm to the Readings
In the first reading Moses talks God into relenting of the punishment unfaithful Israel deserves. In the gospel the prodigal son relents of his sinfulness and is embraced by his father. The Pharisees and scribes, on the
other hand, refuse to relent in their judgment against Jesus for eating
with sinners. The elder son refuses to relent of his resentment at his
prodigal brother and his anger at his forgiving father.

The responsorial psalm for this Sunday, taken from Psalm 51, is our
song of relenting. Through it we align ourselves with the tax collectors
and sinners, with the lost sheep, and with the prodigal son. Such align-

ment is part of the radical gift of self which discipleship demands, for through it we give up any vestige of false self-image. We can be found because we admit that we are lost. We can receive God's unrestricted and limitless mercy because we confess we are in need of it.

Psalmist Preparation

Your singing these verses from Psalm 51 is a public act of confession, for you stand before the assembly and admit sinfulness. But even more importantly, you confess the mercy of God who never spurns a contrite and humbled heart. As you prepare to sing this psalm, what forgiveness might you ask of God? What relenting of sin and pride might you need to do?

Prayer

Merciful God, you seek out those who are lost. When we stray from your side, give us the courage to admit our sinfulness and return to your embrace. We ask this through Christ our Lord. Amen.

Gospel (Luke 16:1-13 [or Luke 16:10-13]; L135C)

Jesus said to his disciples, "A rich man had a steward who was reported to him for squandering his property. He summoned him and said, 'What is this I hear about you? Prepare a full account of your stewardship, because you can no longer be my steward.' The steward said to himself, 'What shall I do, now that my master is taking the position of steward away from me? I am not strong enough to dig and I am ashamed to beg. I know what I shall do so that, when I am removed from the stewardship, they may welcome me into their homes.' He called in his master's debtors one by one. To the first he said, 'How much do you owe my master?' He replied, 'One hundred measures of olive oil.' He said to him, 'Here is your promissory note. Sit down and quickly write one for fifty.' Then to another the steward said, 'And you, how much do you owe?' He replied, 'One hundred kors of wheat.' The steward said to him, 'Here is your promissory note; write one for eighty.' And the master commended that dishonest steward for acting prudently.

"For the children of this world are more prudent in dealing with their own generation than are the children of light. I tell you, make friends for yourselves with dishonest wealth, so that when it fails, you will be welcomed into eternal dwellings. The person who is trustworthy in very small matters is also trustworthy in great ones; and the person who is dishonest in very small matters is also dishonest in great ones. If, therefore, you are not trustworthy with dishonest wealth, who will trust you with true wealth? If you are not trustworthy with what belongs to another, who will give you what is yours? No servant can serve two masters. He will either hate one and love the other, or be devoted to one and despise the other. You cannot serve both God and mammon."

First Reading (Amos 8:4-7)

Hear this, you who trample upon the needy
    and destroy the poor of the land!
"When will the new moon be over," you ask,
    "that we may sell our grain,
    and the sabbath, that we may display the wheat?

We will diminish the ephah,
  add to the shekel,
  and fix our scales for cheating!
We will buy the lowly for silver,
  and the poor for a pair of sandals;
  even the refuse of the wheat we will sell!"
The LORD has sworn by the pride of Jacob:
  Never will I forget a thing they have done!

Responsorial Psalm (Ps 113:1-2, 4-6, 7-8)

R̋. (cf. 1a, 7b) Praise the Lord, who lifts up the poor. *or:* R̋. Alleluia.

Praise, you servants of the LORD,
  praise the name of the LORD.
Blessed be the name of the LORD
  both now and forever.

R̋. Praise the Lord, who lifts up the poor. *or:* R̋. Alleluia.

High above all nations is the LORD;
  above the heavens is his glory.
Who is like the LORD, our God, who is enthroned on high
  and looks upon the heavens and the earth below?

R̋. Praise the Lord, who lifts up the poor. *or:* R̋. Alleluia.

He raises up the lowly from the dust;
  from the dunghill he lifts up the poor
to seat them with princes,
  with the princes of his own people.

R̋. Praise the Lord, who lifts up the poor. *or:* R̋. Alleluia.

Second Reading (1 Tim 2:1-8)

Reflecting on Living the Gospel

This gospel puts to us a basic question: Whom do we serve? The wily steward is clearly self-serving and decisive in doing what he thinks necessary for his own immediate well-being. But by acting in this way, he risks squandering his eternal well-being ("eternal dwellings"). To secure this, he needed to choose to serve God rather than self. The irony is that had he chosen to serve God and God alone, he would have chosen to serve himself in the best way possible.

TWENTY-FIFTH SUNDAY IN ORDINARY TIME

Connecting the Responsorial Psalm to the Readings

It is easy to see a connection between the responsorial psalm and the first reading. In the reading God swears never to forget an injustice done to the poor. In the psalm God redresses such wrongs and raises the poor from dust to nobility.

It is not so easy, however, to detect a connection between the psalm and the gospel. The first reading and the gospel both relate incidences of unjust and dishonest behavior pursued for the sake of personal gain. Jesus condemns the dishonest behavior, yet he commends the dishonest steward for pursuing it. What Jesus invites, however, is not imitation of the behavior but imitation of the shrewdness that motivates it. We must know what we want and act decisively to obtain it. We must desire what is just and true and act in its service. The psalm offers us the model of God who seeks what is just and true and acts decisively to redress wrongs and raise up the poor. To praise this God is to choose our Master.

Psalmist Preparation

In singing this psalm you invite the assembly to praise God for acting on behalf of the poor and oppressed. In the context of the first reading and gospel, you also invite them to imitate God in their own manner of acting. In what ways do you choose God as your Master and guide? In what ways do you struggle with this choice? How might Christ help you?

Prayer

Almighty God, you are worthy of all praise. Teach us to be wise stewards and trustworthy disciples who serve only you. We ask this through Christ our Lord. Amen.

Gospel (Luke 16:19-31; L138C)

Jesus said to the Pharisees: "There was a rich man who dressed in purple garments and fine linen and dined sumptuously each day. And lying at his door was a poor man named Lazarus, covered with sores, who would gladly have eaten his fill of the scraps that fell from the rich man's table. Dogs even used to come and lick his sores. When the poor man died, he was carried away by angels to the bosom of Abraham. The rich man also died and was buried, and from the netherworld, where he was in torment, he raised his eyes and saw Abraham far off and Lazarus at his side. And he cried out, 'Father Abraham, have pity on me. Send Lazarus to dip the tip of his finger in water and cool my tongue, for I am suffering torment in these flames.' Abraham replied, 'My child, remember that you received what was good during your lifetime while Lazarus likewise received what was bad; but now he is comforted here, whereas you are tormented. Moreover, between us and you a great chasm is established to prevent anyone from crossing who might wish to go from our side to yours or from your side to ours.' He said, 'Then I beg you, father, send him to my father's house, for I have five brothers, so that he may warn them, lest they too come to this place of torment.' But Abraham replied, 'They have Moses and the prophets. Let them listen to them.' He said, 'Oh no, father Abraham, but if someone from the dead goes to them, they will repent.' Then Abraham said, 'If they will not listen to Moses and the prophets, neither will they be persuaded if someone should rise from the dead.'"

First Reading (Amos 6:1a, 4-7)

Thus says the LORD, the God of hosts:
Woe to the complacent in Zion!
Lying upon beds of ivory,
    stretched comfortably on their couches,
they eat lambs taken from the flock,
    and calves from the stall!
Improvising to the music of the harp,
    like David, they devise their own accompaniment.

They drink wine from bowls
  and anoint themselves with the best oils;
  yet they are not made ill by the collapse of Joseph!
Therefore, now they shall be the first to go into exile,
  and their wanton revelry shall be done away with.

Responsorial Psalm (Ps 146:7, 8-9, 9-10)

R̞. (1b) Praise the Lord, my soul! *or:* R̞. Alleluia.

Blessed is he who keeps faith forever,
  secures justice for the oppressed,
  gives food to the hungry.
The LORD sets captives free.

R̞. Praise the Lord, my soul! *or:* R̞. Alleluia.

The LORD gives sight to the blind.
  The LORD raises up those who were bowed down.
The LORD loves the just;
  the LORD protects strangers.

R̞. Praise the Lord, my soul! *or:* R̞. Alleluia.

The fatherless and the widow he sustains,
  but the way of the wicked he thwarts.
The LORD shall reign forever;
  your God, O Zion, through all generations. Alleluia.

R̞. Praise the Lord, my soul! *or:* R̞. Alleluia.

Second Reading (1 Tim 6:11-16)

Reflecting on Living the Gospel
The rich man in torment begs Abraham to send "someone from the
dead" to warn his five brothers to repent and change their way of living.
In fact, during his earthly life, the rich man *had* "someone from the dead"
warning him to repent and change—the sick, suffering, starving Lazarus
"lying at his door" who was as good as "dead" to the rich man. Indeed,
"someone from the dead" *has* come to warn us, too. Who? Do we listen?

Connecting the Responsorial Psalm to the Readings
Those who are suffering and in need are beloved by God (gospel, psalm).
If we separate ourselves from the poor and needy, as do the complacent
in the first reading and the rich man in the gospel, we separate ourselves
from God and from the possibility of blessed life in eternity. Had they

heeded Moses and the prophets (gospel), these individuals would have lived differently and secured a different future for themselves. By praising God who is never indifferent to human suffering, Psalm 146 is a message from Moses and the prophets to us. We must do more than merely sing this message, however. We must hear it and heed.

Psalmist Preparation

As with last Sunday's psalm this psalm holds God up as the model of behavior for faithful disciples. Disciples of Jesus are called to act on behalf of the poor and suffering just as God does. In singing this psalm you invite the assembly to respond to this call. In what ways are you responding? In what ways do you need to grow in your response?

Prayer

God of justice, you hear the cry of those who suffer. Open our ears that we may hear this cry and our hearts that we may respond with your mercy. We ask this through Christ our Lord. Amen.

Gospel (Luke 17:5-10; L141C)

The apostles said to the Lord, "Increase our faith." The Lord replied, "If you have faith the size of a mustard seed, you would say to this mulberry tree, 'Be uprooted and planted in the sea,' and it would obey you.

"Who among you would say to your servant who has just come in from plowing or tending sheep in the field, 'Come here immediately and take your place at table'? Would he not rather say to him, 'Prepare something for me to eat. Put on your apron and wait on me while I eat and drink. You may eat and drink when I am finished'? Is he grateful to that servant because he did what was commanded? So should it be with you. When you have done all you have been commanded, say, 'We are unprofitable servants; we have done what we were obliged to do.'"

First Reading (Hab 1:2-3; 2:2-4)

How long, O LORD? I cry for help
    but you do not listen!
I cry out to you, "Violence!"
    but you do not intervene.
Why do you let me see ruin;
    why must I look at misery?
Destruction and violence are before me;
    there is strife, and clamorous discord.
Then the LORD answered me and said:
    Write down the vision clearly upon the tablets,
    so that one can read it readily.
For the vision still has its time,
    presses on to fulfillment, and will not disappoint;
if it delays, wait for it,
    it will surely come, it will not be late.
The rash one has no integrity;
    but the just one, because of his faith, shall live.

Responsorial Psalm (Ps 95:1-2, 6-7, 8-9)

R℣. (8) If today you hear his voice, harden not your hearts.

Come, let us sing joyfully to the LORD;
    let us acclaim the Rock of our salvation.

Let us come into his presence with thanksgiving;
   let us joyfully sing psalms to him.

R℣. If today you hear his voice, harden not your hearts.

Come, let us bow down in worship;
   let us kneel before the LORD who made us.
For he is our God,
   and we are the people he shepherds, the flock he guides.

R℣. If today you hear his voice, harden not your hearts.

Oh, that today you would hear his voice:
   "Harden not your hearts as at Meribah,
   as in the day of Massah in the desert,
where your fathers tempted me;
   they tested me though they had seen my works."

R℣. If today you hear his voice, harden not your hearts.

Second Reading (2 Tim 1:6-8, 13-14)

Reflecting on Living the Gospel

Jesus says that even faith "the size of a mustard seed" is enough to do
great things. The "unprofitable servants" of Jesus' gospel teaching simply do what they are commanded—they do not go beyond normal expectations; they cannot uproot a mulberry tree. To go beyond expectations,
we must risk doing the impossible and thereby become profitable servants. In this we align ourselves with God, become able to do as God
does. Being aligned with God: this is faith.

Connecting the Responsorial Psalm to the Readings

Psalm 95, like other psalms such as Psalm 15, includes a ritual for entrance into the temple for worship. Before being admitted the people
were asked if they had been faithful to God who created and shepherded
them. The question was no idle one, for many of Israel's ancestors had
not been permitted entrance into the Promised Land because of their infidelity. This is the story behind verses 8-9, and the reason for the harsh
words in the refrain, "harden not your hearts." Faith means following the
vision God lays before us (first reading). Faith means doing what God
expects of us (gospel). Faith means acting according to who we are,
God's chosen people (psalm). Faith means aligning ourselves with God in
a way that transforms our hearts and our behavior.

Psalmist Preparation

The harsh shift between the beginning of this responsorial psalm and its conclusion only makes sense when you know the story behind the psalm. The psalm reminds you, and the assembly, that true worship includes fidelity to God's commands. When are you tempted to turn away from the demands of fidelity? What helps your heart hear God's voice and remain faithful?

Prayer

Ever-faithful God, you are steadfast in keeping your promises. When our confidence in you wavers and our energy for discipleship flags, keep us steadfast in our promises to you. We ask this through Christ our Lord. Amen.

Gospel (Luke 17:11-19; L144C)

As Jesus continued his journey to Jerusalem, he traveled through Samaria and Galilee. As he was entering a village, ten lepers met him. They stood at a distance from him and raised their voices, saying, "Jesus, Master! Have pity on us!" And when he saw them, he said, "Go show yourselves to the priests." As they were going they were cleansed. And one of them, realizing he had been healed, returned, glorifying God in a loud voice; and he fell at the feet of Jesus and thanked him. He was a Samaritan. Jesus said in reply, "Ten were cleansed, were they not? Where are the other nine? Has none but this foreigner returned to give thanks to God?" Then he said to him, "Stand up and go; your faith has saved you."

First Reading (2 Kgs 5:14-17)

Naaman went down and plunged into the Jordan seven times at the word of Elisha, the man of God. His flesh became again like the flesh of a little child, and he was clean of his leprosy.

Naaman returned with his whole retinue to the man of God. On his arrival he stood before Elisha and said, "Now I know that there is no God in all the earth, except in Israel. Please accept a gift from your servant."

Elisha replied, "As the LORD lives whom I serve, I will not take it"; and despite Naaman's urging, he still refused. Naaman said: "If you will not accept, please let me, your servant, have two mule-loads of earth, for I will no longer offer holocaust or sacrifice to any other god except to the LORD."

Responsorial Psalm (Ps 98:1, 2-3, 3-4)

℟. (cf. 2b) The Lord has revealed to the nations his saving power.

Sing to the LORD a new song,
for he has done wondrous deeds;
his right hand has won victory for him,
his holy arm.

℟. The Lord has revealed to the nations his saving power.

The LORD has made his salvation known:
in the sight of the nations he has revealed his justice.
He has remembered his kindness and his faithfulness
toward the house of Israel.

R⁊. The Lord has revealed to the nations his saving power.

All the ends of the earth have seen
the salvation by our God.
Sing joyfully to the LORD, all you lands:
break into song; sing praise.

R⁊. The Lord has revealed to the nations his saving power.

Second Reading (2 Tim 2:8-13)

Reflecting on Living the Gospel

The ten lepers were all outcasts. Jesus, on his journey to Jerusalem which
would end in salvation for all, healed them all. For Jesus, there are no
outcasts. Yet only one of the ten demonstrates that being saved is being
healed, is returning to the Healer, is glorifying God, is falling at the feet
of Jesus, is giving thanks. Only one shows us *how* faith saves. Faith is
not static; it is dynamic, unfolding in concrete acts of response, praise,
worship, and thanksgiving.

Connecting the Responsorial Psalm to the Readings

Psalm 98, from which this Sunday's responsorial psalm is taken, sings
about the completion of God's salvific plan for Israel. All the forces
which threaten God's chosen people—depicted in various psalms as
enemy nations, roaring seas, evildoers, famine, disease—have been put
to rout by God. God's "wondrous deeds" of salvation have been revealed,
and the whole world rejoices. The healing stories in the first reading and
gospel are concrete dramatizations of God's saving deeds. By singing
Psalm 98 we join Naaman and the grateful leper in offering thanks to
God for saving us from disease and death. We express our faith in God
and are granted salvation.

Psalmist Preparation

Reflect this week on where you have seen God's salvation unfold—in
your own life, in the church, in the world. Let your singing of this responsorial psalm be both a proclamation of God's deeds and a thanksgiving for them.

Prayer

God of salvation, you overcome all that keeps us from fullness of life. Fill our hearts with gratitude and our lips with songs of praise that we may make your saving work known to all the world. We ask this through Christ our Lord. Amen.

TWENTY-NINTH SUNDAY IN ORDINARY TIME

Gospel (Luke 18:1-8; L147C)

Jesus told his disciples a parable about the necessity for them to pray always without becoming weary. He said, "There was a judge in a certain town who neither feared God nor respected any human being. And a widow in that town used to come to him and say, 'Render a just decision for me against my adversary.' For a long time the judge was unwilling, but eventually he thought, 'While it is true that I neither fear God nor respect any human being, because this widow keeps bothering me I shall deliver a just decision for her lest she finally come and strike me.'" The Lord said, "Pay attention to what the dishonest judge says. Will not God then secure the rights of his chosen ones who call out to him day and night? Will he be slow to answer them? I tell you, he will see to it that justice is done for them speedily. But when the Son of Man comes, will he find faith on earth?"

First Reading (Exod 17:8-13)

In those days, Amalek came and waged war against Israel. Moses, therefore, said to Joshua, "Pick out certain men, and tomorrow go out and engage Amalek in battle. I will be standing on top of the hill with the staff of God in my hand." So Joshua did as Moses told him: he engaged Amalek in battle after Moses had climbed to the top of the hill with Aaron and Hur. As long as Moses kept his hands raised up, Israel had the better of the fight, but when he let his hands rest, Amalek had the better of the fight. Moses' hands, however, grew tired; so they put a rock in place for him to sit on. Meanwhile Aaron and Hur supported his hands, one on one side and one on the other, so that his hands remained steady till sunset. And Joshua mowed down Amalek and his people with the edge of the sword.

Responsorial Psalm (Ps 121:1-2, 3-4, 5-6, 7-8)

R̚. (cf. 2) Our help is from the Lord, who made heaven and earth.

I lift up my eyes toward the mountains;
    whence shall help come to me?
My help is from the LORD,
    who made heaven and earth.

R̚. Our help is from the Lord, who made heaven and earth.

May he not suffer your foot to slip;
    may he slumber not who guards you:
indeed he neither slumbers nor sleeps,
    the guardian of Israel.

R̦. Our help is from the Lord, who made heaven and earth.

The LORD is your guardian; the LORD is your shade;
    he is beside you at your right hand.
The sun shall not harm you by day,
    nor the moon by night.

R̦. Our help is from the Lord, who made heaven and earth.

The LORD will guard you from all evil;
    he will guard your life.
The LORD will guard your coming and your going,
    both now and forever.

R̦. Our help is from the Lord, who made heaven and earth.

Second Reading (2 Tim 3:14–4:2)

Reflecting on Living the Gospel

The widow seeks justice out of need; the judge renders justice out of exasperation; God bestows justice out of love for God's "chosen ones / who call out to him day and night." The widow had a legal relationship with the judge that ended the moment he rendered a decision. We, however, have a personal relationship with God that continually deepens as we "pray always," that reveals we are God's "chosen ones" who are in right relationship with God.

Connecting the Responsorial Psalm to the Readings

Psalm 121, used in its entirety this Sunday, is a pilgrimage song. Having journeyed to Jerusalem for festival, the Israelites must now travel home. They see the dark mountains which surround them as a threat, the hideout of thieves and enemies, the home of wild animals. The psalm is a prayer of confidence in God's protection, perhaps said in blessing over them by the temple priest as the pilgrims begin their journey home. What motivates the prayer is surety about God. The Israelites know that God answers the prayer of those who are faithful to the covenant. Moses had such confidence (first reading) as did Jesus (gospel), as do we when we sing this psalm. May our singing reveal the "faith on earth" the Son of Man longs to find when he returns (gospel).

Psalmist Preparation

When you sing this responsorial psalm, you are like the temple priest blessing the people as they begin their journey homeward. The people are the Body of Christ, the journey that of faithful discipleship, the homeland God's kingdom. How will your singing assure the assembly of God's Presence and protection on the way?

Prayer

Creator of heaven and earth, you guard our comings and goings as we journey heavenward. Keep us safe from evil, sure in our footing along the path of discipleship, and faithful to you every step of our way. We ask this through Christ our Lord. Amen.

Gospel (Luke 18:9-14; L150C)

Jesus addressed this parable to those who were convinced of their own righteousness and despised everyone else. "Two people went up to the temple area to pray; one was a Pharisee and the other was a tax collector. The Pharisee took up his position and spoke this prayer to himself, 'O God, I thank you that I am not like the rest of humanity— greedy, dishonest, adulterous—or even like this tax collector. I fast twice a week, and I pay tithes on my whole income.' But the tax collector stood off at a distance and would not even raise his eyes to heaven but beat his breast and prayed, 'O God, be merciful to me a sinner.' I tell you, the latter went home justified, not the former; for whoever exalts himself will be humbled, and the one who humbles himself will be exalted."

First Reading (Sir 35:12-14, 16-18)

The LORD is a God of justice,
   who knows no favorites.
Though not unduly partial toward the weak,
   yet he hears the cry of the oppressed.
The LORD is not deaf to the wail of the orphan,
   nor to the widow when she pours out her complaint.
The one who serves God willingly is heard;
   his petition reaches the heavens.
The prayer of the lowly pierces the clouds;
   it does not rest till it reaches its goal,
nor will it withdraw till the Most High responds,
   judges justly and affirms the right,
and the LORD will not delay.

Responsorial Psalm (Ps 34:2-3, 17-18, 19, 23)

R℣. The Lord hears the cry of the poor.

I will bless the LORD at all times;
   his praise shall be ever in my mouth.
Let my soul glory in the LORD;
   the lowly will hear me and be glad.

R℣. The Lord hears the cry of the poor.

The Lord confronts the evildoers,
  to destroy remembrance of them from the earth.
When the just cry out, the Lord hears them,
  and from all their distress he rescues them.

R̸. The Lord hears the cry of the poor.

The Lord is close to the brokenhearted;
  and those who are crushed in spirit he saves.
The Lord redeems the lives of his servants;
  no one incurs guilt who takes refuge in him.

R̸. The Lord hears the cry of the poor.

Second Reading (2 Tim 4:6-8, 16-18)

Reflecting on Living the Gospel

Both the Pharisee and tax collector addressed God in prayer. The content
of their prayer, however, differed greatly. The Pharisee's prayer was
about himself and was turned toward self. The tax collector's prayer, by
contrast, was turned toward God in the true self-knowledge of who he
was. Jesus declared the tax collector justified, not the Pharisee. Justifica-
tion—right relationship with God—comes only from knowing ourselves
as God knows us. Paradoxically, true humility is exaltation—the gift received while being one's true self before God and others.

Connecting the Responsorial Psalm to the Readings

It is not the self-righteous whom God hears in prayer (gospel) but those
"crushed in spirit" (responsorial psalm). God is not close-minded to the
rich; indeed, God "knows no favorites" (first reading). Rather, it is that
the self-satisfied are closed to God. Only those who recognize their need
for mercy can see and receive the action of God on their behalf. In this
Sunday's responsorial psalm we identify ourselves with the poor, the brokenhearted, the lowly. We acknowledge our right relationship with
God—that of dependency, of humility, and of a need for mercy. Out of
this attitude we pray, and God hears us.

Psalmist Preparation

The words of the responsorial psalm parallel the message Jesus tells in
his parable of the Pharisee and the tax collector (gospel). When you sing
these words, then, you know what Jesus knew, and you tell it. What was
it that Jesus knew?

Prayer

God of justice, you hear the cry of the poor and the petition of the lowly. Help us always to stand humbly before you that you may raise us up in glory. We ask this through Christ our Lord. Amen.

Gospel (Luke 19:1-10; L153C)

At that time, Jesus came to Jericho and intended to pass through the town. Now a man there named Zacchaeus, who was a chief tax collector and also a wealthy man, was seeking to see who Jesus was; but he could not see him because of the crowd, for he was short in stature. So he ran ahead and climbed a sycamore tree in order to see Jesus, who was about to pass that way. When he reached the place, Jesus looked up and said, "Zacchaeus, come down quickly, for today I must stay at your house." And he came down quickly and received him with joy. When they all saw this, they began to grumble, saying, "He has gone to stay at the house of a sinner." But Zacchaeus stood there and said to the Lord, "Behold, half of my possessions, Lord, I shall give to the poor, and if I have extorted anything from anyone I shall repay it four times over." And Jesus said to him, "Today salvation has come to this house because this man too is a descendant of Abraham. For the Son of Man has come to seek and to save what was lost."

First Reading (Wis 11:22–12:2)

Before the LORD the whole universe is as a grain from a balance
    or a drop of morning dew come down upon the earth.
But you have mercy on all, because you can do all things;
    and you overlook people's sins that they may repent.
For you love all things that are
    and loathe nothing that you have made;
    for what you hated, you would not have fashioned.
And how could a thing remain, unless you willed it;
    or be preserved, had it not been called forth by you?
But you spare all things, because they are yours,
    O LORD and lover of souls,
    for your imperishable spirit is in all things!
Therefore you rebuke offenders little by little,
    warn them and remind them of the sins
      they are committing,
    that they may abandon their wickedness
      and believe in you, O LORD!

Responsorial Psalm **(Ps 145:1-2, 8-9, 10-11, 13, 14)**

℟. (cf. 1) I will praise your name forever, my king and my God.

I will extol you, O my God and King,
   and I will bless your name forever and ever.
Every day will I bless you,
   and I will praise your name forever and ever.

℟. I will praise your name forever, my king and my God.

The LORD is gracious and merciful,
   slow to anger and of great kindness.
The LORD is good to all
   and compassionate toward all his works.

℟. I will praise your name forever, my king and my God.

Let all your works give you thanks, O LORD,
   and let your faithful ones bless you.
Let them discourse of the glory of your kingdom
   and speak of your might.

℟. I will praise your name forever, my king and my God.

The LORD is faithful in all his words
   and holy in all his works.
The LORD lifts up all who are falling
   and raises up all who are bowed down.

℟. I will praise your name forever, my king and my God.

Second Reading (2 Thess 1:11–2:2)

Reflecting on Living the Gospel

Zacchaeus's short stature kept him from seeing Jesus with his physical eyes. His ardent desire to encounter Jesus, however, indicates that he had already seen him with the eyes of his heart. Encountering Jesus does not depend upon the goodness of one's life, but encountering him can bring about conversion of life. Zacchaeus chooses to put his life in right order. For this does Zacchaeus come to salvation. We come to salvation when we see Jesus with the eyes of our own hearts wide open.

Connecting the Responsorial Psalm to the Readings

Psalm 145 is an acrostic hymn, meaning that each verse begins with a successive letter of the Hebrew alphabet. Consequently, the psalm does not develop any theme in depth but simply offers God general praise. The verses chosen for this Sunday praise God for showing mercy and compassion rather than anger, and for lifting up those who have fallen. The reading from Wisdom confirms this attitude of God when it proclaims that the Lord "overlooks people's sins" and gently coaxes offenders back to right living. Clearly God prefers reconciliation to condemnation.

In his encounter with Zacchaeus Jesus is the living embodiment of this orientation of God (gospel). Jesus "has come to seek / and to save what was lost" (gospel). In singing this psalm we are the living embodiment of Zacchaeus's response. We recognize ourselves as sinners and shout praise to the One who comes to change and save us.

Psalmist Preparation

Psalm 145 praises God for all that God does, but in the context of the first reading and gospel the praise is particularly for God's mercy to sinners. For what have you been shown this mercy? How have you praised God for it?

Prayer

Gracious and merciful God, you seek out the lost and draw them back to your loving embrace. May we always seek you, opening our hearts to your mercy and graciously receiving the salvation you offer. We ask this through Christ our Lord. Amen.

Gospel (Matt 5:1-12a; L667)

When Jesus saw the crowds, he went up the mountain, and after he had sat down, his disciples came to him. He began to teach them, saying:

"Blessed are the poor in spirit,
for theirs is the Kingdom of heaven.
Blessed are they who mourn,
for they will be comforted.
Blessed are the meek,
for they will inherit the land.
Blessed are they who hunger and thirst for righteousness,
for they will be satisfied.
Blessed are the merciful,
for they will be shown mercy.
Blessed are the clean of heart,
for they will see God.
Blessed are the peacemakers,
for they will be called children of God.
Blessed are they who are persecuted for the sake of righteousness,
for theirs is the Kingdom of heaven.

Blessed are you when they insult you and persecute you and utter every kind of evil against you falsely because of me. Rejoice and be glad, for your reward will be great in heaven."

First Reading (Rev 7:2-4, 9-14)

I, John, saw another angel come up from the East, holding the seal of the living God. He cried out in a loud voice to the four angels who were given power to damage the land and the sea, "Do not damage the land or the sea or the trees until we put the seal on the foreheads of the servants of our God." I heard the number of those who had been marked with the seal, one hundred and forty-four thousand marked from every tribe of the children of Israel.

After this I had a vision of a great multitude, which no one could count, from every nation, race, people, and tongue. They stood before the throne and before the Lamb, wearing white robes and holding palm branches in their hands. They cried out in a loud voice:

"Salvation comes from our God,
who is seated on the throne,
and from the Lamb."

All the angels stood around the throne and around the elders and the four living creatures. They prostrated themselves before the throne, worshiped God, and exclaimed:

"Amen. Blessing and glory, wisdom and thanksgiving,
honor, power, and might
be to our God forever and ever. Amen."

Then one of the elders spoke up and said to me, "Who are these wearing white robes, and where did they come from?" I said to him, "My lord, you are the one who knows." He said to me, "These are the ones who have survived the time of great distress; they have washed their robes and made them white in the Blood of the Lamb."

Responsorial Psalm (Ps 24:1-2, 3-4, 5-6)

R̸. Lord, this is the people that longs to see your face.

The LORD's are the earth and its fullness;
the world and those who dwell in it.
For he founded it upon the seas
and established it upon the rivers.

R̸. Lord, this is the people that longs to see your face.

Who can ascend the mountain of the LORD?
or who may stand in his holy place?
One whose hands are sinless, whose heart is clean,
who desires not what is vain.

R̸. Lord, this is the people that longs to see your face.

He shall receive a blessing from the LORD,
a reward from God his savior.
Such is the race that seeks for him,
that seeks the face of the God of Jacob.

R̸. Lord, this is the people that longs to see your face.

See Appendix, p. 217, for Second Reading

Reflecting on Living the Gospel

Jesus *"began* to teach" his disciples the Beatitudes, an ongoing way of living for his followers. Disciples' learning is not only in the hearing, but even more importantly in the daily living. The saints we honor today are those who took Jesus' Beatitudes to heart and lived them well. They now dwell in the land of inheritance—"the Kingdom of heaven" where they "see God" and know the fullness of what it means to be called "blessed."

Connecting the Responsorial Psalm to the Readings

Psalm 24 is one of the psalms of ascent. As the Israelites traveled to Jerusalem for solemn festival they raised their eyes to the "mountain of the LORD." Upon arrival at the temple door, they were questioned, "Who can ascend [this] mountain . . . who may stand in [this] holy place?" They then responded, "One whose hands are sinless, whose heart is clean, / who desires not what is vain." These are the very qualities Jesus spells out in the Beatitudes (gospel). The Israelites were faithful to the law and the covenant because they knew they were God's chosen people. We live the Beatitudes because we know we are God's children (second reading). With the Israelites, we long to see God's face (psalm refrain). With all those who are faithful to this longing, we reap the reward of heaven.

Psalmist Preparation

The first psalm strophe tells of God's power, the last of God's blessings upon those who are faithful. The middle strophe describes those who are faithful. In singing this psalm you speak sometimes to God, sometimes to the people. Pray that you may speak to both with humility and love.

Prayer

Good and gracious God, you bestow upon us great love, calling us your own children. Teach us to live always as your holy ones, faithful to your ways of blessedness. We ask this through Christ our Lord. Amen.

Gospel (Luke 20:27-38 [or Luke 20:27, 34-38]; L156C)

Some Sadducees, those who deny that there is a resurrection, came forward and put this question to Jesus, saying, "Teacher, Moses wrote for us, *If someone's brother dies leaving a wife but no child, his brother must take the wife and raise up descendants for his brother.* Now there were seven brothers; the first married a woman but died childless. Then the second and the third married her, and likewise all the seven died childless. Finally the woman also died. Now at the resurrection whose wife will that woman be? For all seven had been married to her." Jesus said to them, "The children of this age marry and remarry; but those who are deemed worthy to attain to the coming age and to the resurrection of the dead neither marry nor are given in marriage. They can no longer die, for they are like angels; and they are the children of God because they are the ones who will rise. That the dead will rise even Moses made known in the passage about the bush, when he called out 'Lord,' the God of Abraham, the God of Isaac, and the God of Jacob; and he is not God of the dead, but of the living, for to him all are alive."

First Reading (2 Macc 7:1-2, 9-14)

It happened that seven brothers with their mother were arrested and tortured with whips and scourges by the king, to force them to eat pork in violation of God's law. One of the brothers, speaking for the others, said: "What do you expect to achieve by questioning us? We are ready to die rather than transgress the laws of our ancestors."

At the point of death he said: "You accursed fiend, you are depriving us of this present life, but the King of the world will raise us up to live again forever. It is for his laws that we are dying."

After him the third suffered their cruel sport. He put out his tongue at once when told to do so, and bravely held out his hands, as he spoke these noble words: "It was from Heaven that I received these; for the sake of his laws I disdain them; from him I hope to receive them again." Even the king and his attendants marveled at the young man's courage, because he regarded his sufferings as nothing.

After he had died, they tortured and maltreated the fourth brother in the same way. When he was near death, he said, "It is my choice to die at the hands of men with the hope God gives of being raised up by him; but for you, there will be no resurrection to life."

Responsorial Psalm (Ps 17:1, 5-6, 8, 15)

℟. (15b) Lord, when your glory appears, my joy will be full.

Hear, O LORD, a just suit;
    attend to my outcry;
    hearken to my prayer from lips without deceit.

℟. Lord, when your glory appears, my joy will be full.

My steps have been steadfast in your paths,
    my feet have not faltered.
I call upon you, for you will answer me, O God;
    incline your ear to me; hear my word.

℟. Lord, when your glory appears, my joy will be full.

Keep me as the apple of your eye,
    hide me in the shadow of your wings.
But I in justice shall behold your face;
    on waking I shall be content in your presence.

℟. Lord, when your glory appears, my joy will be full.

Second Reading (2 Thess 2:16–3:5)

Reflecting on Living the Gospel
For the Sadducees, one's immortality was contingent on having progeny, the tradition and context of their argument about marrying and remarrying taken to extremes. Jesus answers them by asserting that there is no marriage and remarriage in heaven because there is no dying in heaven. In heaven, "all are alive," in perfect union with God. The proof of Jesus' truth is his own resurrection, his own perfect union with his Father. The promise of Jesus' truth is our resurrection, our perfect union with God.

Connecting the Responsorial Psalm to the Readings
On this Sunday when the church begins to focus on the end times and the Second Coming of Christ, both the first reading and the gospel speak directly of God's promise to raise the just to new life after death. The martyred brothers in the first reading remain faithful to the covenant even to death, for they believe that the Giver of life and limb will never take back what has been bestowed. Jesus in the gospel asserts "the dead will rise," for God is God "of the living."

    Like the brothers, Jesus knows that he will be put to death for remaining faithful to the call of God. In the responsorial psalm we align ourselves with Jesus. We state our hope that on "waking" from death we shall find ourselves in the presence of God. And we make a commitment that we will remain "steadfast in [the] paths" of discipleship. As we celebrate this Eucharist and sing this psalm, we look to the glory of Christ to come and know that we shall share in that glory just as we have shared in its price.

Psalmist Preparation

In this responsorial psalm you proclaim your faith in God's promise of eternal life and your choice to remain faithful to discipleship no matter what it costs. This is no small thing considering the cost will be your life. What conversation might you have with Christ this week to give you courage and strengthen your hope?

Prayer

God of the living, you promise everlasting life to those who are faithful to you. Let us see now the glory you have in store for us that we may be strengthened in our fidelity to you. We ask this through Christ our Lord. Amen.

Gospel (Luke 21:5-19; L159C)

While some people were speaking about how the temple was adorned with costly stones and votive offerings, Jesus said, "All that you see here— the days will come when there will not be left a stone upon another stone that will not be thrown down."

Then they asked him, "Teacher, when will this happen? And what sign will there be when all these things are about to happen?" He answered, "See that you not be deceived, for many will come in my name, saying, 'I am he,' and 'The time has come.' Do not follow them! When you hear of wars and insurrections, do not be terrified; for such things must happen first, but it will not immediately be the end." Then he said to them, "Nation will rise against nation, and kingdom against kingdom. There will be powerful earthquakes, famines, and plagues from place to place; and awesome sights and mighty signs will come from the sky.

"Before all this happens, however, they will seize and persecute you, they will hand you over to the synagogues and to prisons, and they will have you led before kings and governors because of my name. It will lead to your giving testimony. Remember, you are not to prepare your defense beforehand, for I myself shall give you a wisdom in speaking that all your adversaries will be powerless to resist or refute. You will even be handed over by parents, brothers, relatives, and friends, and they will put some of you to death. You will be hated by all because of my name, but not a hair on your head will be destroyed. By your perseverance you will secure your lives."

First Reading (Mal 3:19-20a)

Lo, the day is coming, blazing like an oven,
  when all the proud and all evildoers will be stubble,
and the day that is coming will set them on fire,
  leaving them neither root nor branch,
  says the LORD of hosts.
But for you who fear my name, there will arise
  the sun of justice with its healing rays.

Responsorial Psalm (Ps 98:5-6, 7-8, 9)

℞. (cf. 9) The Lord comes to rule the earth with justice.

Sing praise to the LORD with the harp,
  with the harp and melodious song.
With trumpets and the sound of the horn
  sing joyfully before the King, the LORD.

℞. The Lord comes to rule the earth with justice.

Let the sea and what fills it resound,
  the world and those who dwell in it;
let the rivers clap their hands,
  the mountains shout with them for joy.

℞. The Lord comes to rule the earth with justice.

Before the LORD, for he comes,
  for he comes to rule the earth;
he will rule the world with justice
  and the peoples with equity.

℞. The Lord comes to rule the earth with justice.

Second Reading (2 Thess 3:7-12)

Reflecting on Living the Gospel

In the beginning, all things came to be. At the end, things as we know them will cease to be. Does anything really last forever? Certainly not temples, not nations, not even the foundations of the earth. So, what does last forever? God, the wisdom of Jesus, divine Life. And, yes, the lives of those who persevere in fidelity to the name and mission of Jesus and who "will secure" a share in divine Life. At the end . . . a new beginning.

Connecting the Responsorial Psalm to the Readings

In the context of this Sunday's first reading and gospel, Psalm 98 is a statement of absolute certainty that the power of Christ will prevail over the forces of evil. We need not lose heart when wars, insurrections, earthquakes, famines arise. We need not be surprised when fidelity to discipleship brings persecution. Even amidst the direst evil, the vision we maintain is of Christ's final coming and victory. And so we sing, blow trumpets, clap hands, and shout for joy, for we know the Lord is coming to rule with justice.

Psalmist Preparation

When you sing this responsorial psalm, you stand before the assembly testifying to a vision of the future in which God reigns with justice. Do you believe in this future? Are you looking for it? Will you stake your life on it?

Prayer

God of power and might, you have promised to send your Son to the nations with justice and salvation. As we await the day of his coming, keep us courageous in discipleship and persevering in hope. We ask this in his name. Amen.

Gospel (Luke 23:35-43; L162C)

The rulers sneered at Jesus and said, "He saved others, let him save himself if he is the chosen one, the Christ of God." Even the soldiers jeered at him. As they approached to offer him wine they called out, "If you are King of the Jews, save yourself." Above him there was an inscription that read, "This is the King of the Jews."

Now one of the criminals hanging there reviled Jesus, saying, "Are you not the Christ? Save yourself and us." The other, however, rebuking him, said in reply, "Have you no fear of God, for you are subject to the same condemnation? And indeed, we have been condemned justly, for the sentence we received corresponds to our crimes, but this man has done nothing criminal." Then he said, "Jesus, remember me when you come into your kingdom." He replied to him, "Amen, I say to you, today you will be with me in Paradise."

First Reading (2 Sam 5:1-3)

In those days, all the tribes of Israel came to David in Hebron and said: "Here we are, your bone and your flesh. In days past, when Saul was our king, it was you who led the Israelites out and brought them back. And the LORD said to you, 'You shall shepherd my people Israel and shall be commander of Israel.'" When all the elders of Israel came to David in Hebron, King David made an agreement with them there before the LORD, and they anointed him king of Israel.

Responsorial Psalm (Ps 122:1-2, 3-4, 4-5)

R̸. (cf. 1) Let us go rejoicing to the house of the Lord.

I rejoiced because they said to me,
  "We will go up to the house of the LORD."
And now we have set foot
  within your gates, O Jerusalem.

R̸. Let us go rejoicing to the house of the Lord.

Jerusalem, built as a city
  with compact unity.

To it the tribes go up,
the tribes of the LORD.

R℣. Let us go rejoicing to the house of the Lord.

According to the decree for Israel,
to give thanks to the name of the LORD.
In it are set up judgment seats,
seats for the house of David.

R℣. Let us go rejoicing to the house of the Lord.

See Appendix, p. 217, for Second Reading

Reflecting on Living the Gospel

Three hang on crosses, suffering and dying. One reviles, one begs for salvation, One promises Paradise. Indeed, only *One* can promise Paradise. Who but "the Christ of God" could make such a promise? Who but a divine King could reach beyond his own suffering and dying to bestow Life on another? Who but One totally innocent of evil could draw goodness out of one who is "condemned justly"? Three hang on crosses. One remains condemned. One is redeemed. One will rise from the dead, King of the universe.

Connecting the Responsorial Psalm to the Readings

Israelites arriving at the gates of Jerusalem for annual worship sang Psalm 122. It was a song of great joy, for entering Jerusalem meant encountering God. It meant celebrating membership in God's people. It meant reaffirming who they were and who God was for them. On this Solemnity of Christ the King we, too, celebrate who we are and who God is for us. We are the people forgiven by God through Christ's redeeming death (second reading). We are the very "bone" and "flesh" (first reading) of Christ, members of the Body of which he is the Head (second reading). We are the ones remembered by Christ and called by him into Paradise (gospel). Let us enter with rejoicing!

Psalmist Preparation

In singing this responsorial psalm you invite the assembly to enter the kingdom of God. They have journeyed through all of Ordinary Time. They have struggled, they have been faithful. Bring them in with joy.

OUR LORD JESUS CHRIST, KING OF THE UNIVERSE

Prayer

Lord, Jesus Christ, in you all fullness dwells, all reconciliation is completed, all peace is granted. Lead us with joy into the kingdom of your presence and our glory. We ask this in humility and hope. Amen.

APPENDIX

FIRST SUNDAY OF ADVENT, November 29, 2015
Second Reading (1 Thess 3:12–4:2)
Brothers and sisters: May the Lord make you increase and abound in love for one another and for all, just as we have for you, so as to strengthen your hearts, to be blameless in holiness before our God and Father at the coming of our Lord Jesus with all his holy ones. Amen.

Finally, brothers and sisters, we earnestly ask and exhort you in the Lord Jesus that, as you received from us how you should conduct yourselves to please God—and as you are conducting yourselves—you do so even more. For you know what instructions we gave you through the Lord Jesus.

SECOND SUNDAY OF ADVENT, December 6, 2015
Second Reading (Phil 1:4-6, 8-11)
Brothers and sisters: I pray always with joy in my every prayer for all of you, because of your partnership for the gospel from the first day until now. I am confident of this, that the one who began a good work in you will continue to complete it until the day of Christ Jesus. God is my witness, how I long for all of you with the affection of Christ Jesus. And this is my prayer: that your love may increase ever more and more in knowledge and every kind of perception, to discern what is of value, so that you may be pure and blameless for the day of Christ, filled with the fruit of righteousness that comes through Jesus Christ for the glory and praise of God.

THE IMMACULATE CONCEPTION OF THE BLESSED VIRGIN MARY, December 8, 2015
Second Reading (Eph 1:3-6, 11-12)
Brothers and sisters: Blessed be the God and Father of our Lord Jesus Christ, who has blessed us in Christ with every spiritual blessing in the heavens, as he chose us in him, before the foundation of the world, to be holy and without blemish before him. In love he destined us for adoption to himself through Jesus Christ, in accord with the favor of his will, for the praise of the glory of his grace that he granted us in the beloved.

In him we were also chosen, destined in accord with the purpose of the One who accomplishes all things according to the intention of his will, so that we might exist for the praise of his glory, we who first hoped in Christ.

THIRD SUNDAY OF ADVENT, December 13, 2015
Second Reading (Phil 4:4-7)
Brothers and sisters: Rejoice in the Lord always. I shall say it again: rejoice! Your kindness should be known to all. The Lord is near. Have no anxiety at all, but in everything, by prayer and petition, with thanksgiving, make your requests known to God. Then the peace of God that surpasses all understanding will guard your hearts and minds in Christ Jesus.

FOURTH SUNDAY OF ADVENT, December 20, 2015
Second Reading (Heb 10:5-10)

Brothers and sisters: When Christ came into the world, he said:

> "Sacrifice and offering you did not desire,
> but a body you prepared for me;
> in holocausts and sin offerings you took no delight.
> Then I said, 'As is written of me in the scroll,
> behold, I come to do your will, O God.'"

First he says, "Sacrifices and offerings, holocausts and sin offerings, you neither desired nor delighted in." These are offered according to the law. Then he says, "Behold, I come to do your will." He takes away the first to establish the second. By this "will," we have been consecrated through the offering of the body of Jesus Christ once for all.

THE NATIVITY OF THE LORD, *Vigil Mass*, December 24, 2015
Second Reading (Acts 13:16-17, 22-25)

When Paul reached Antioch in Pisidia and entered the synagogue, he stood up, motioned with his hand, and said, "Fellow Israelites and you others who are God-fearing, listen. The God of this people Israel chose our ancestors and exalted the people during their sojourn in the land of Egypt. With uplifted arm he led them out of it. Then he removed Saul and raised up David as king; of him he testified, 'I have found David, son of Jesse, a man after my own heart; he will carry out my every wish.' From this man's descendants God, according to his promise, has brought to Israel a savior, Jesus. John heralded his coming by proclaiming a baptism of repentance to all the people of Israel; and as John was completing his course, he would say, 'What do you suppose that I am? I am not he. Behold, one is coming after me; I am not worthy to unfasten the sandals of his feet.'"

THE NATIVITY OF THE LORD, *Mass at Midnight*, December 25, 2015
Second Reading (Titus 2:11-14)

Beloved: The grace of God has appeared, saving all and training us to reject godless ways and worldly desires and to live temperately, justly, and devoutly in this age, as we await the blessed hope, the appearance of the glory of our great God and savior Jesus Christ, who gave himself for us to deliver us from all lawlessness and to cleanse for himself a people as his own, eager to do what is good.

THE NATIVITY OF THE LORD, *Mass at Dawn*, December 25, 2015
Second Reading (Titus 3:4-7)

Beloved:
> When the kindness and generous love
>   of God our savior appeared,
> not because of any righteous deeds we had done
>   but because of his mercy,
> he saved us through the bath of rebirth
>   and renewal by the Holy Spirit,
> whom he richly poured out on us
>   through Jesus Christ our savior,
> so that we might be justified by his grace
>   and become heirs in hope of eternal life.

THE NATIVITY OF THE LORD, *Mass During the Day,* **December 25, 2015**
Second Reading **(Heb 1:1-6)**
Brothers and sisters: In times past, God spoke in partial and various ways to our
ancestors through the prophets; in these last days, he has spoken to us through the
Son, whom he made heir of all things and through whom he created the universe,

who is the refulgence of his glory, the very imprint of his being,
and who sustains all things by his mighty word.
When he had accomplished purification from sins,
he took his seat at the right hand of the Majesty on high,
as far superior to the angels
as the name he has inherited is more excellent than theirs.

For to which of the angels did God ever say:

You are my son; this day I have begotten you?

Or again:

I will be a father to him, and he shall be a son to me?

And again, when he leads the firstborn into the world, he says:

Let all the angels of God worship him.

THE HOLY FAMILY OF JESUS, MARY, AND JOSEPH, December 27, 2015
Second Reading **(1 John 3:1-2, 21-24 [or Col 3:12-21 or Col 3:12-17])**
Beloved: See what love the Father has bestowed on us that we may be called the
children of God. And so we are. The reason the world does not know us is that it
did not know him. Beloved, we are God's children now; what we shall be has not
yet been revealed. We do know that when it is revealed we shall be like him, for
we shall see him as he is.

Beloved, if our hearts do not condemn us, we have confidence in God and
receive from him whatever we ask, because we keep his commandments and do
what pleases him. And his commandment is this: we should believe in the name
of his Son, Jesus Christ, and love one another just as he commanded us. Those
who keep his commandments remain in him, and he in them, and the way we
know that he remains in us is from the Spirit he gave us.

SOLEMNITY OF MARY, THE HOLY MOTHER OF GOD,
January 1, 2016
Second Reading **(Gal 4:4-7)**
Brothers and sisters: When the fullness of time had come, God sent his Son, born
of a woman, born under the law, to ransom those under the law, so that we might
receive adoption as sons. As proof that you are sons, God sent the Spirit of his
Son into our hearts, crying out, "Abba, Father!" So you are no longer a slave but a
son, and if a son then also an heir, through God.

THE EPIPHANY OF THE LORD, January 3, 2016
Second Reading (Eph 3:2-3a, 5-6)

Brothers and sisters: You have heard of the stewardship of God's grace that was given to me for your benefit, namely, that the mystery was made known to me by revelation. It was not made known to people in other generations as it has now been revealed to his holy apostles and prophets by the Spirit: that the Gentiles are coheirs, members of the same body, and copartners in the promise in Christ Jesus through the gospel.

THE BAPTISM OF THE LORD, January 10, 2016
Second Reading (Titus 2:11-14; 3:4-7 [or Acts 10:34-38])

Beloved: The grace of God has appeared, saving all and training us to reject godless ways and worldly desires and to live temperately, justly, and devoutly in this age, as we await the blessed hope, the appearance of the glory of our great God and savior Jesus Christ, who gave himself for us to deliver us from all lawlessness and to cleanse for himself a people as his own, eager to do what is good.

> When the kindness and generous love
>   of God our savior appeared,
> not because of any righteous deeds we had done
>   but because of his mercy,
> he saved us through the bath of rebirth
>   and renewal by the Holy Spirit,
> whom he richly poured out on us
>   through Jesus Christ our savior,
> so that we might be justified by his grace
>   and become heirs in hope of eternal life.

ASH WEDNESDAY, February 10, 2016
Second Reading (2 Cor 5:20–6:2)

Brothers and sisters: We are ambassadors for Christ, as if God were appealing through us. We implore you on behalf of Christ, be reconciled to God. For our sake he made him to be sin who did not know sin, so that we might become the righteousness of God in him.

Working together, then, we appeal to you not to receive the grace of God in vain. For he says:

> *In an acceptable time I heard you,*
>   *and on the day of salvation I helped you.*

Behold, now is a very acceptable time; behold, now is the day of salvation.

FIRST SUNDAY OF LENT, February 14, 2016
Second Reading (Rom 10:8-13)

Brothers and sisters: What does Scripture say?

> *The word is near you,*
> *in your mouth and in your heart*

—that is, the word of faith that we preach—, for, if you confess with your mouth that Jesus is Lord and believe in your heart that God raised him from the dead, you will be saved. For one believes with the heart and so is justified, and one confesses with the mouth and so is saved. For the Scripture says, *No one who believes in him will be put to shame.* For there is no distinction between Jew and Greek; the same Lord is Lord of all, enriching all who call upon him. For "everyone who calls on the name of the Lord will be saved."

SECOND SUNDAY OF LENT, February 21, 2016
Second Reading (Phil 3:17–4:1 [or Phil 3:20–4:1])

Join with others in being imitators of me, brothers and sisters, and observe those who thus conduct themselves according to the model you have in us. For many, as I have often told you and now tell you even in tears, conduct themselves as enemies of the cross of Christ. Their end is destruction. Their God is their stomach; their glory is in their "shame." Their minds are occupied with earthly things. But our citizenship is in heaven, and from it we also await a savior, the Lord Jesus Christ. He will change our lowly body to conform with his glorified body by the power that enables him also to bring all things into subjection to himself.

Therefore, my brothers and sisters, whom I love and long for, my joy and crown, in this way stand firm in the Lord.

THIRD SUNDAY OF LENT, February 28, 2016
Second Reading (1 Cor 10:1-6, 10-12)

I do not want you to be unaware, brothers and sisters, that our ancestors were all under the cloud and all passed through the sea, and all of them were baptized into Moses in the cloud and in the sea. All ate the same spiritual food, and all drank the same spiritual drink, for they drank from a spiritual rock that followed them, and the rock was the Christ. Yet God was not pleased with most of them, for they were struck down in the desert.

These things happened as examples for us, so that we might not desire evil things, as they did. Do not grumble as some of them did, and suffered death by the destroyer. These things happened to them as an example, and they have been written down as a warning to us, upon whom the end of the ages has come. Therefore, whoever thinks he is standing secure should take care not to fall.

FOURTH SUNDAY OF LENT, March 6, 2016
Second Reading (2 Cor 5:17-21)

Brothers and sisters: Whoever is in Christ is a new creation: the old things have passed away; behold, new things have come. And all this is from God, who has reconciled us to himself through Christ and given us the ministry of reconciliation, namely, God was reconciling the world to himself in Christ, not counting their trespasses against them and entrusting to us the message of reconciliation. So we are ambassadors for Christ, as if God were appealing through us. We implore you on behalf of Christ, be reconciled to God. For our sake he made him to be sin who did not know sin, so that we might become the righteousness of God in him.

FIFTH SUNDAY OF LENT, March 13, 2016
Second Reading (Phil 3:8-14)

Brothers and sisters: I consider everything as a loss because of the supreme good of knowing Christ Jesus my Lord. For his sake I have accepted the loss of all things and I consider them so much rubbish, that I may gain Christ and be found in him, not having any righteousness of my own based on the law but that which comes through faith in Christ, the righteousness from God, depending on faith to know him and the power of his resurrection and the sharing of his sufferings by being conformed to his death, if somehow I may attain the resurrection from the dead.

It is not that I have already taken hold of it or have already attained perfect maturity, but I continue my pursuit in hope that I may possess it, since I have indeed been taken possession of by Christ Jesus. Brothers and sisters, I for my part do not consider myself to have taken possession. Just one thing: forgetting what lies behind but straining forward to what lies ahead, I continue my pursuit toward the goal, the prize of God's upward calling, in Christ Jesus.

PALM SUNDAY OF THE LORD'S PASSION, March 20, 2016
Second Reading (Phil 2:6-11)

Christ Jesus, though he was in the form of God,
    did not regard equality with God
    something to be grasped.
Rather, he emptied himself,
    taking the form of a slave,
    coming in human likeness;
    and found human in appearance,
    he humbled himself,
    becoming obedient to the point of death,
    even death on a cross.
Because of this, God greatly exalted him
    and bestowed on him the name
    which is above every name,
    that at the name of Jesus
    every knee should bend,
    of those in heaven and on earth and under the earth,
    and every tongue confess that
    Jesus Christ is Lord,
    to the glory of God the Father.

HOLY THURSDAY EVENING MASS OF THE LORD'S SUPPER,
March 24, 2016
Second Reading (1 Cor 11:23-26)
Brothers and sisters: I received from the Lord what I also handed on to you, that the Lord Jesus, on the night he was handed over, took bread, and, after he had given thanks, broke it and said, "This is my body that is for you. Do this in remembrance of me." In the same way also the cup, after supper, saying, "This cup is the new covenant in my blood. Do this, as often as you drink it, in remembrance of me." For as often as you eat this bread and drink the cup, you proclaim the death of the Lord until he comes.

FRIDAY OF THE LORD'S PASSION (Good Friday), March 25, 2016
Second Reading (Heb 4:14-16; 5:7-9)
Brothers and sisters: Since we have a great high priest who has passed through the heavens, Jesus, the Son of God, let us hold fast to our confession. For we do not have a high priest who is unable to sympathize with our weaknesses, but one who has similarly been tested in every way, yet without sin. So let us confidently approach the throne of grace to receive mercy and to find grace for timely help.

In the days when Christ was in the flesh, he offered prayers and supplications with loud cries and tears to the one who was able to save him from death, and he was heard because of his reverence. Son though he was, he learned obedience from what he suffered; and when he was made perfect, he became the source of eternal salvation for all who obey him.

EASTER SUNDAY OF THE RESURRECTION, March 27, 2016
Second Reading (1 Cor 5:6b-8 [or Col 3:1-4])
Brothers and sisters: Do you not know that a little yeast leavens all the dough? Clear out the old yeast, so that you may become a fresh batch of dough, inasmuch as you are unleavened. For our paschal lamb, Christ, has been sacrificed. Therefore, let us celebrate the feast, not with the old yeast, the yeast of malice and wickedness, but with the unleavened bread of sincerity and truth.

SECOND SUNDAY OF EASTER (or of Divine Mercy), April 3, 2016
Second Reading (Rev 1:9-11a, 12-13, 17-19)
I, John, your brother, who share with you the distress, the kingdom, and the endurance we have in Jesus, found myself on the island called Patmos because I proclaimed God's word and gave testimony to Jesus. I was caught up in spirit on the Lord's day and heard behind me a voice as loud as a trumpet, which said, "Write on a scroll what you see." Then I turned to see whose voice it was that spoke to me, and when I turned, I saw seven gold lampstands and in the midst of the lampstands one like a son of man, wearing an ankle-length robe, with a gold sash around his chest.

When I caught sight of him, I fell down at his feet as though dead. He touched me with his right hand and said, "Do not be afraid. I am the first and the last, the one who lives. Once I was dead, but now I am alive forever and ever. I hold the keys to death and the netherworld. Write down, therefore, what you have seen, and what is happening, and what will happen afterwards."

THIRD SUNDAY OF EASTER, April 10, 2016
Second Reading (Rev 5:11-14)

I, John, looked and heard the voices of many angels who surrounded the throne and the living creatures and the elders. They were countless in number, and they cried out in a loud voice:

> "Worthy is the Lamb that was slain
> > to receive power and riches, wisdom and strength,
> > honor and glory and blessing."

Then I heard every creature in heaven and on earth and under the earth and in the sea, everything in the universe, cry out:

> "To the one who sits on the throne and to the Lamb
> > be blessing and honor, glory and might,
> > forever and ever."

The four living creatures answered, "Amen," and the elders fell down and worshiped.

FOURTH SUNDAY OF EASTER, April 17, 2016
Second Reading (Rev 7:9, 14b-17)

I, John, had a vision of a great multitude, which no one could count, from every nation, race, people, and tongue. They stood before the throne and before the Lamb, wearing white robes and holding palm branches in their hands.

Then one of the elders said to me, "These are the ones who have survived the time of great distress; they have washed their robes and made them white in the blood of the Lamb.

> "For this reason they stand before God's throne
> > and worship him day and night in his temple.
> The one who sits on the throne will shelter them.
> They will not hunger or thirst anymore,
> > nor will the sun or any heat strike them.
> For the Lamb who is in the center of the throne
> > will shepherd them
> > and lead them to springs of life-giving water,
> > and God will wipe away every tear from their eyes."

FIFTH SUNDAY OF EASTER, April 24, 2016
Second Reading (Rev 21:1-5a)

Then I, John, saw a new heaven and a new earth. The former heaven and the former earth had passed away, and the sea was no more. I also saw the holy city, a new Jerusalem, coming down out of heaven from God, prepared as a bride adorned for her husband. I heard a loud voice from the throne saying, "Behold, God's dwelling is with the human race. He will dwell with them and they will be his people and God himself will always be with them as their God. He will wipe every tear from their eyes, and there shall be no more death or mourning, wailing or pain, for the old order has passed away."

The One who sat on the throne said, "Behold, I make all things new."

SIXTH SUNDAY OF EASTER, May 1, 2016
Second Reading (Rev 21:10-14, 22-23)

The angel took me in spirit to a great, high mountain and showed me the holy city Jerusalem coming down out of heaven from God. It gleamed with the splendor of God. Its radiance was like that of a precious stone, like jasper, clear as crystal. It had a massive, high wall, with twelve gates where twelve angels were stationed and on which names were inscribed, the names of the twelve tribes of the Israelites. There were three gates facing east, three north, three south, and three west. The wall of the city had twelve courses of stones as its foundation, on which were inscribed the twelve names of the twelve apostles of the Lamb.

I saw no temple in the city for its temple is the Lord God almighty and the Lamb. The city had no need of sun or moon to shine on it, for the glory of God gave it light, and its lamp was the Lamb.

THE ASCENSION OF THE LORD, May 5 or 8, 2016
Second Reading (Eph 1:17-23 [or Heb 9:24-28; 10:19-23])

Brothers and sisters: May the God of our Lord Jesus Christ, the Father of glory, give you a Spirit of wisdom and revelation resulting in knowledge of him. May the eyes of your hearts be enlightened, that you may know what is the hope that belongs to his call, what are the riches of glory in his inheritance among the holy ones, and what is the surpassing greatness of his power for us who believe, in accord with the exercise of his great might, which he worked in Christ, raising him from the dead and seating him at his right hand in the heavens, far above every principality, authority, power, and dominion, and every name that is named not only in this age but also in the one to come. And he put all things beneath his feet and gave him as head over all things to the church, which is his body, the fullness of the one who fills all things in every way.

SEVENTH SUNDAY OF EASTER, May 8, 2016
Second Reading (Rev 22:12-14, 16-17, 20)

I, John, heard a voice saying to me: "Behold, I am coming soon. I bring with me the recompense I will give to each according to his deeds. I am the Alpha and the Omega, the first and the last, the beginning and the end."

Blessed are they who wash their robes so as to have the right to the tree of life and enter the city through its gates.

"I, Jesus, sent my angel to give you this testimony for the churches. I am the root and offspring of David, the bright morning star."

The Spirit and the bride say, "Come." Let the hearer say, "Come." Let the one who thirsts come forward, and the one who wants it receive the gift of life-giving water.

The one who gives this testimony says, "Yes, I am coming soon." Amen! Come, Lord Jesus!

PENTECOST SUNDAY, May 15, 2016
Second Reading (Rom 8:8-17 [or I Cor 12:3b-7, 12-13])

Brothers and sisters: Those who are in the flesh cannot please God. But you are not in the flesh; on the contrary, you are in the spirit, if only the Spirit of God dwells in you. Whoever does not have the Spirit of Christ does not belong to him. But if Christ is in you, although the body is dead because of sin, the spirit is alive because of righteousness. If the Spirit of the one who raised Jesus from the dead dwells in you, the one who raised Christ from the dead will give life to your mortal bodies also, through his Spirit that dwells in you. Consequently, brothers and sisters, we are not debtors to the flesh, to live according to the flesh. For if you live according to the flesh, you will die, but if by the Spirit you put to death the deeds of the body, you will live.

For those who are led by the Spirit of God are sons of God. For you did not receive a spirit of slavery to fall back into fear, but you received a Spirit of adoption, through whom we cry, "Abba, Father!" The Spirit himself bears witness with our spirit that we are children of God, and if children, then heirs, heirs of God and joint heirs with Christ, if only we suffer with him so that we may also be glorified with him.

THE SOLEMNITY OF THE MOST HOLY TRINITY, May 22, 2016
Second Reading (Rom 5:1-5)

Brothers and sisters: Therefore, since we have been justified by faith, we have peace with God through our Lord Jesus Christ, through whom we have gained access by faith to this grace in which we stand, and we boast in hope of the glory of God. Not only that, but we even boast of our afflictions, knowing that affliction produces endurance, and endurance, proven character, and proven character, hope, and hope does not disappoint, because the love of God has been poured out into our hearts through the Holy Spirit that has been given to us.

THE SOLEMNITY OF THE MOST HOLY BODY AND BLOOD OF CHRIST, May 29, 2016
Second Reading (I Cor 11:23-26)

Brothers and sisters: I received from the Lord what I also handed on to you, that the Lord Jesus, on the night he was handed over, took bread, and, after he had given thanks, broke it and said, "This is my body that is for you. Do this in remembrance of me." In the same way also the cup, after supper, saying, "This cup is the new covenant in my blood. Do this, as often as you drink it, in remembrance of me." For as often as you eat this bread and drink the cup, you proclaim the death of the Lord until he comes.

THE ASSUMPTION OF THE BLESSED VIRGIN MARY, August 15, 2016
Second Reading (1 Cor 15:20-27)

Brothers and sisters: Christ has been raised from the dead, the firstfruits of those who have fallen asleep. For since death came through man, the resurrection of the dead came also through man. For just as in Adam all die, so too in Christ shall all be brought to life, but each one in proper order: Christ the firstfruits; then, at his coming, those who belong to Christ; then comes the end, when he hands over the Kingdom to his God and Father, when he has destroyed every sovereignty and every authority and power. For he must reign until he has put all his enemies under his feet. The last enemy to be destroyed is death, for "he subjected everything under his feet."

ALL SAINTS, November 1, 2016
Second Reading (1 John 3:1-3)

Beloved: See what love the Father has bestowed on us that we may be called the children of God. Yet so we are. The reason the world does not know us is that it did not know him. Beloved, we are God's children now; what we shall be has not yet been revealed. We do know that when it is revealed we shall be like him, for we shall see him as he is. Everyone who has this hope based on him makes himself pure, as he is pure.

THE SOLEMNITY OF OUR LORD JESUS CHRIST, KING OF THE UNIVERSE, November 20, 2016
Second Reading (Col 1:12-20)

Brothers and sisters: Let us give thanks to the Father, who has made you fit to share in the inheritance of the holy ones in light. He delivered us from the power of darkness and transferred us to the kingdom of his beloved Son, in whom we have redemption, the forgiveness of sins.

He is the image of the invisible God,
    the firstborn of all creation.
For in him were created all things in heaven and on earth,
    the visible and the invisible,
        whether thrones or dominions or principalities or powers;
    all things were created through him and for him.
He is before all things,
    and in him all things hold together.
He is the head of the body, the church.
He is the beginning, the firstborn from the dead,
    that in all things he himself might be preeminent.
For in him all the fullness was pleased to dwell,
    and through him to reconcile all things for him,
    making peace by the blood of his cross
    through him, whether those on earth or those in heaven.